TAKE AIM and FLAME

FOCUSING YOUR ZEAL AND STIRRING YOUR THRILL FOR CHRIST

TONYA BUCK BENNETT

WESTBOW
PRESS

A DIVISION OF THOMAS NELSON

All Scripture quotations are taken from Life Application Study Bible, New International Version. Copyright 1988, 1989, 1990, 1991, 2005 by Tyndale House Publishers, Inc., and Zondervan.

WestBow Press books may be ordered through booksellers or by contacting:

WestBow Press
A Division of Thomas Nelson
1663 Liberty Drive
Bloomington, IN 47403
www.westbowpress.com
1-(866) 928-1240

ISBN: 978-1-4497-4261-4 (sc)
ISBN: 978-1-4497-4260-7 (e)

Library of Congress Control Number: 2012904087

Printed in the United States of America

WestBow Press rev. date: 03/20/2012

To the ones who desire to live life more passionately,
even in the face of difficulty, and honor God more powerfully.

——Acknowledgments

To my daughters, Kayla and Kelsey: I hope you will always know how much I love being your mom. My prayer for you both is to "shine like stars in the universe as you hold out the word of life" (Phil 2:15-16). To my husband, Everett, and my parents, Carolyn and William: I could never thank you enough for your support through my sickness. When I felt like giving up, your endless love gave me relentless determination to take aim and flame for Christ!

CONTENTS

In everyone's life, at some time, our inner fire goes out. It is then burst into flame by an encounter with another human being. We should all be thankful for those people who rekindle the inner spirit.

Albert Schweitzer

CHAPTER 1

A Dimly Burning Flame

Move with me into the dimly burning wick's heart. Overwhelmed with pain. Consumed with drain. Can't sleep from an overworked brain. Rejected with a stain. Fed up with the mundane. Bitter because of memory lane. Frustrated by the restrain. On the edge of insane. Hello? Can I get a witness? Is there anybody out there who can relate to any of these eight? Oh man, I can!

You see, no matter the age, Satan blows with a gigantic rage to put out your flame and hinder your aim to serve Christ with an unbridled passion. With my bow steady and my arrow ready, I'm aiming this thought right toward you. So don't duck. It's time you get out of the muck.

Listen closely. As long as you're filled with despair, you're out of Satan's hair. When you lose God's perspective, you're less effective. If the enemy can get you stuck in the confused zone, he will keep you from flaming on with vitality and fortitude. The enemy really fears what will happen when you get a belly full of fire that will not expire in the face of adversity.

Precious one, dimly burning wicks fill the Bible. And if you are going to do anything with greatness for God to be glorified, you will experience this dimly burning wick's heart at some point.

GRAB A SEAT AND LET'S TALK ABOUT HEAT

Are you hot or not? Be honest. Are you brimming over with zeal or feeling quite a chill when it comes to sharing your passion for Christ

1

with others? Well, I'm going to be honest. I can't tell you how many times I have recently cried, "Lord, please come quick and breathe upon this dimly burning wick!" No matter how long you have been serving God, there are times when you just bury your head in your hands and cry out the words of Psalm 6:3, "How long, O LORD, how long?" I'm so glad the book of Isaiah has good news. "A bruised reed He will not break, and a smoldering wick he will not snuff out" (Isa 42:3).

Even when it seems life's struggles have just about taken all the fire out of you, God, in His supremacy, knows exactly what to do. He fans what He plans! God knows just how to rekindle what we think is dead back to a fiery red.

In Romans 4:17, Paul encourages us that God "gives life to the dead and calls things that are not as though they were." Tender one, your flame is not dead! It's just getting qualified to be widespread. Here's the way I see it. What you call "dead," God sees as an "arrowhead" with limitless potential to be launched out to minister to hurting people. My earnest desire is for God to use this book to help you become more effective as a fiery tool in kingdom ministry.

Speaking of tools, let's take a side journey to Exodus 27:1-3, where it speaks of useful tools formed of bronze for the altar of burnt offering. Like a worm in hot ashes, I squirm every time I read this scripture. Why? Because I see exactly what type of tool I want to be. "Make all its utensils of bronze—it's pots to remove the ashes, its shovels, sprinkling bowls, meat forks and firepans." There it is. "Oh, Lord, fan your plan until Tonya Bennett becomes an effective firepan!" I can't allow my flame to cool if I'm going to be a fiery tool. Oh, how I long to be a utensil that is used for carrying hot fire to the world. I want to be in the spot that is zealously hot. There's no doubt about it, folks. God wants us deeply drawn to a face-to-face encounter with Him. He wants us to know His heart, His character, and His fiery love.

As you walk through the pages of this book, I pray you will acquire a fresh fire that refuses to burn out in the season of sufferings. The fact is that we all struggle, get weary, and face the temptation to burn out. Adversity will often cause you to stop believing and achieving your goal to move forward with holy determination. Oh, boy, I know this one well.

Can I get a little personal here? Medical records offer this ol' girl little hope of seeing God-given dreams come to fruition. So what do

I do? Pout and reroute my aim to a pity party? I think not! For when you're sold out, you can't take the easy route. I choose to keep a "yes face" in a "no place." I choose to bust for my must, which is to share "the good news of the kingdom of God" (Luke 4:43). I choose to rest in the shadow of His wings until this disaster has passed (Ps 57:1). In that place, God reminds me that he created my "mouth like a sharpened sword, in the shadow of his hand he hid me; he made me into a polished arrow and concealed me in his quiver" (Isa 49:2). My heart's desire is be an arrow that is unstoppable.

I don't care how many stacks of medical reports say, "Nope!" With my God, there is always hope and confidence that He will fulfill every single purpose that He has for my life. I just keep telling myself, "My eyes will see what my fiery heart desires." I hope this book will encourage you to pronounce those same blessings over your dreams and situations.

You see, what we see as chaos and commotion, God sees as a divine promotion into kingdom ministry. My desire to take aim and flame will not rely on circumstances or medical records. My challenges will have to submit to the plans of God. And so will yours.

Don't settle for darkness. God has more. His promise is found in Psalm 112:4. "Even in darkness light dawns for the upright." Yes, it would be really nice if life were all about brownies and hot fudge instead of having to trudge through the tough stuff. But in the hard times, I think about Paul. Like this apostle, I refuse to "run aimlessly" (1 Cor 9:26). I choose to grab a hold of Psalms and run with it in the palms of my hands as I declare, "But the plans of the LORD stand firm forever" (Ps 33:11).

Sometimes, the pain from trials is so difficult that all I know to do is sit in silence and cry, "God, I love you!" And it never fails. Jesus's words found in Psalm 91:14 bubbles up inside of me. "'Because he loves me,' says the Lord, 'I will rescue him; I will protect him, for he acknowledges my name. He will call upon me, and I will answer him; I will be with him in trouble, I will deliver him and honor him. With long life will I satisfy him and show him my salvation.'" What a promise!

Maybe you are experiencing layers of darkness right now. In fact, you might not be able to see the sun because of a dark cloud. So for you, I will share this idea really loud! You were created for greatness! You were created to be a stepping-stone to help another person aim on!

This is a given. Learning to take aim and flame doesn't just happen. Rather, it is an active, determined, steady resolve in which the archer stands at the firing line with the right equipment, form, and established anchor point in which to release the targeted arrows. Your equipment and form must be founded upon God's Word. Your anchor point is always founded on the Father's love. Every day, God longs to train us how to set our eyes on His target, depend upon His sufficiency, and exclaim our love for Him.

For crying out loud, it's time we become real with Jesus. Be transparent. He already knows how you feel anyway. He's God. If you're frustrated, He can take it. If you doubt, He can shake it. If your flame is dimly burning, he can make it flame higher than what you could ever imagine! However, you must see the need to desperately cry out. You were created for volume. So, let it out. Cry out to Him with desperate passion.

Oh, this is what I love about my Father. He truly understands that every archer's finger will get sore and lose grip of the arrow. Therefore, Jesus runs to the cry of His beloved. He establishes your feet in a stance position, curls your fingers around the bowstring with His strength, and tenderly guides your eyes until they are fixed back on the center of His plans, His higher ways, His eternal view, and His purpose-filled target.

Oh, how I pray the message in this book stirs you to a place the enemy never intended you to go, a place where you can grow, glow, and overflow for Christ with a new fiery aim. Don't settle for the dimly burning wick. God wants to see you become a high-rising flame with a determined aim to allow Him to use you however He chooses.

Oooh! I'm squirming again because what He chooses might not be too comfortable. But deep down, the ultimate cry of my heart is for God to take the route in my life that brings Him the greatest glory.

More and more, I want to echo the words of Paul, "I consider my life worth nothing to me, if only I may finish the race and complete the task the Lord Jesus has given me—the task of testifying to the gospel of God's grace" (Acts 20:24).

Man, I'm so thrilled. I'm really not trying to get all in your face and all in your space. I just can't help but to be an excited electron that longs to push you to a higher level. I want this book to empower you. I want it to stir something inside of you that screams at the face of every trial,

"No matter the feeling, I am willing to keep my bow and arrow targeted toward God's intentions for my life. My eye is fixed on being a flame for Christ." Together, I believe we can push to the burning bush. I don't want this to be just another book to view. I want the words in this book to push you to the blue.

Hold on now. I didn't say I wanted to make you feel blue. Hang with me here. I believe this book can challenge you to something new. We must press through to reach the blue, the hottest part of a flame.

How can we pursue this blue? Put on your lab coat as we head for a science note. Did you know that a blue flame in a fire comes from excited molecules? Oh, stop! That's the problem right there. Excitement. Difficult seasons often push our excited feet from the fiery seat.

An unknown author once asked a powerful question, "If you are not as close to God as you used to be, who moved?" Ooh! What a thought to ponder! So what do you think? Have you moved the excited flame? Have you chosen a route that has blown out your fire? Leviticus 6:12 says, "The fire on the altar must be kept burning; it must not go out." Did you catch that?

Let me give it a different spin. Your fire was never meant to black out, back out, drop out, fall out, or answer "over and out" to your Creator. Your intense was never meant to be condensed. You were created to blaze out, not phase out.

No matter what flavor of adversity life shoves down my throat, I have no excuse to reduce my heat for the One whose grace is enough for whatever I face. Can I get a loud "Hallelujah"? Anybody with me here? I'm just going to keep hammering this thought until it's caught. Your flame is such a gift that God wants to lift to a new level. When this sinks in, it will burst from within. Then all of a sudden . . . Bam! You won't be able to contain your fiery drive and unquenchable thrive to flame for Christ! Oh, I'm on the edge of my seat writing this thought!

I want this thing to stick to our rib so we'll take off the bib, climb out of the crib, and refuse to believe any fib that the enemy feeds us. Somehow, God will make that hard thing work out for your good and His glory.

I can't emphasize this enough. Don't allow your present circumstances to tempt you into thinking that God has abandoned you. He loves you with an unending love, and He has amazing plans for you to be a fiery flame. Read my lips. You are the pick to be an expansive wick. Dry rot is not going to feel your spot. Got it?

Now, swallow this thought, and let it permeate your spirit. God has a fiery plan designed just for you. However, it will take a titanic determination on your part to trust God during those times when you haven't got a clue what God is doing. Not a clue!

Pardon me for a moment, but sometimes I just have to shout this thought out really loud. "I absolutely refuse to back up, hang up, or toss up my unwavering decision to finish this race with a set aim to flame. I'm going to buckle up and cuddle up to Christ so I can walk out all of His intentions for my life!" Whew! I feel better!

Now, are you fired up from the floor up? I hope so! Read on!

STAY IN THAT SEAT AND DON'T RETREAT

Satan would like nothing better than for you to retreat from your destiny seat. Uh, too late, Tonya. I've already shut that vision gate. Good golly, Miss Molly. You have to open the gate back up and watch God touch up, build up, and line up circumstances to make those God-given dreams happen. I'm telling you. God can do it!

No matter the report or even lack of support that you feel right now, nothing can thwart God's plans for your life if you will cooperate with Him and be patient until He brings everything He has promised you to pass. Oh, Tonya, did you have to use that word "patient"? Yep, I'm afraid so. Everything God has shown you will manifest itself if you aim toward the light and hang on tight with great patience.

Satan cringes at the thought that you would keep aiming and flaming with loyalty to the Father, no matter what you face. Satan starts to sweat when you refuse to fret because of challenges. I am learning to quote Psalm 131:2, "But I have stilled and quieted my soul." Satan wants you to retreat with cold feet from doubt, disbelief, and impatience. So how do we refuse to withdraw from the adversary's gnaw to give up? By keeping a tight grip on God's Word!

In 2 Samuel 23:9, we see that "the men of Israel retreated" when facing their enemy. However, Eleazar, whose very name means "God is helper," refused to retreat. The Word tells us Eleazar "stood his ground and struck down the Philistines till his hand grew tired and froze to the sword" (2 Sam 23:10). Just as Eleazar slayed his enemy in the natural, as a mighty archer, we can come against our enemy in the spirit by keeping our hand fixed on God's infallible Word. As a flame, we must stay on our knees and consistently freeze our hand to His promises.

Every archer knows that you should never fire a bow without an arrow. Else, you will damage or break the bow. If we attempt to aim at any target without God's Word, our effort is useless.

Friend, please don't retreat when affliction comes. Remember this. Nothing you have lost will quench your flame if you fix your eyes on the mighty name, Jesus Christ. That is exactly what Abraham did. In Genesis 22, we find where Abraham lifted up his eyes. He didn't allow the tough and rough to snuff out his flame. Abraham didn't know what God was up to when he was asked to sacrifice his son, Isaac. Though he didn't have a clue, Abraham chose to pursue the blue. Abraham's mind was made up to set aim and flame. He wasn't going to retreat from that promised seat of blessings.

Abraham was a friend of God. According to christian-resources-today.com, Kathryn Hulme once said, "Never forget that God tests his real friends more severely than his lukewarm ones." I believe God's loyal friends won't bend to life's struggles. God's intimates have learned the power of trusting His timing and walking moment by moment by His guidance. Instead of running ahead of God, haphazardly shooting arrows or just simply giving up, they long to listen intently to His daily direction. They are drawn to stand as a light with great height. How ironic that the meaning of Abram is "father of height."

What about you? Have you decided to position one foot on each side of the shooting line with God's intentions in mind? I pray right now that you will picture your arrow of blue as I remind you that your frame was created to take aim! Close your eyes for a minute as you point to yourself and say, "My frame was created to take aim and flame for God!" Get some attitude with it. Shake your head a little bit so the empowerment will transmit.

To the Father, it must be so appetizing when you and I begin realizing that we have an amazing destiny. Like the kingdom of God, the flame "is within you" (Luke 17:21). As a sojourner, you weren't designed to be a church member with a dying ember. Are you getting this, sister? Are you digesting this, brother? You were created to connect with the body of Christ to be an infected carrier of enthusiasm for Jesus. Oh, how I long to sneeze a disease called "to please Christ."

According to thinkexist.com, Billy Graham once said, "Churchgoers are like coals in a fire. When they cling together, they keep the flame aglow; when they separate, they die out." As a unified body, I pray that we hear the battle cry to glorify and amplify our decision to aim for Christ. We can't afford to retreat and miss out on the seat of creative ideas and amazing plans God has for us. When you feel like a dimly burning wick, grab hold of the wisdom from heaven found in Romans 12:11. "Never be lacking in zeal, but keep your spiritual fervor, serving the Lord."

Folks, we have a special position in the kingdom of God. Jesus paid a great price that we could take aim and flame for Him. Just as a candle wick receives a special deposit of wax coating to stay lit, God has "put His Spirit in our hearts as a deposit, guaranteeing what is to come" (2 Cor 1:22).

Let's get intentional to flame! Let's get involved with a steady resolve. Let's fuel our passion by walking in God's fashion with the purpose to ignite and excite others to the love of Christ.

A BLOW WILL SET YOU UP FOR A GLOW

Trials are definitely not fun, but you can sure learn a ton from adversity. Right now, you may feel like your ministry is growing dim. Can I suggest that you raise your candle for a wick trim? Ask God to show you any depleted areas in your life that He wants to oxygenate. I promise you this. God has your spiritual oxygen mask to help you complete your God-given tasks.

Please don't ever think that you're all alone or others aren't experiencing overwhelming challenges. Oh, gosh, that's hogwash. And I fell for it, too. But I've come out of my misery college with some newfound knowledge. Oh, how I burn to share a breath of fresh air everywhere!

You see, it's certain to happen. Every one of us will find ourselves in a desert place like Elijah. Bless his heart. He was sitting under a broom tree of weariness (1 Kgs 19:4). I've been there, done that! But here's what I've learned. If I choose to take aim and flame, despite my feelings, I can step out from under the broom tree and step up under the kaboom tree. Then I can profoundly live out God's purposes of being a resplendent light for Him. And others will notice. Oh, yes, they will. And they will begin to ask you about your insurmountable hope in Christ. Oh, wow, and in that moment, you catch a glimpse of a renewed you and that beautiful flame of blue.

Hear this thought clearly. Though suffering may strip, it will always equip you for greater things. Good gracious, it's not easy to admit this, but it's true. Situations in which I once considered a tough blow have only served to help me grow more dependent upon the sweet Holy Spirit.

Trials will either bury you or carry you to a higher level. Problems will either come between or cause you to lean on Christ. Lean, hun, lean! We must quit looking at challenges as a setback but rather a setup for new God-given opportunities. Together, we can renew and pursue the blue flame as a team. I firmly believe God wants us to grow together so we will glow together and be a light to the nations. After all, the Word says, "Ask of me, and I will make the nations your inheritance, the ends of the earth your possession" (Ps 2:8).

I would really like to encourage you to do a group study with this book. If you are feeling bored or ignored or just have a big void in your life, get ready! You are about to cross over a threshold of new fire. You can't find a better deal to seal than the appeal to take aim and flame for the one who gave His all for you.

Will you join me right now in giving this study to God through prayer? As we unite, we can develop a strong appetite to be a powerful insight to the lost.

In Jesus's name, Father I ask you to cause this book to be a breakthrough to something new. I'm talking big things, Father. I'm asking for the blue as I partner with You. I want the hottest part of the flame that will bring fame to Your name. Please cause the pages of this book to stir and spur us to love You deeply. I am filled with anticipation and expectation to the brim. I dedicate this study with my new buddy in Christ solely to You. We humble ourselves right now so you can awaken any dimly burning wick that exists. Help us to see that you created us to take aim and flame with passion for You. I thank you in advance for the great light expanse. In Jesus's name, I ask this! Amen!

Now, someone strike a match and get ready for heaven's dispatch of encouraging words to fan your flame to have a greater aim.

Bible Study Ideas

Preparation[1]

For the first Bible study night, you will play an icebreaker game. The group leader should record scriptures on a small slip of paper. Then separate the scriptures in half. Make sure you have enough scripture for each member. If both men and women are in the Bible study, make sure you label a cup with "men scripture" and a cup with "women scripture" so men will be paired with men and women with women for the "chat session."

Line up men on one side and women on the other. Randomly pass out the halves of scriptures to each person. Now, get up and get moving. Find the person whose other half matches your scripture. Once you find him or her, you should have a chat session. You must tell your partner things about yourself in which he or she does not already know. When time is called, come back as a group, share your scripture, introduce your partner, and tell something new about your friend to your group.

Direct

Share with your group a highlighted thought that ministered to you.

Reflect

- Did you find yourself in the dimly burning wick's heart? If comfortable, share how.
- Who are some examples of people in the Bible who had a "dimly burning wick's heart"? What did they do about it?
- A fire is put out by removing the heat, oxygen, and fuel. To you, what spiritually represents heat in your life? How does Satan try to put out your heat?
- What spiritually represents oxygen to you?
- What is your fuel?
- Life grows out of life's blows. Can you give an example of this statement in your own life?
- Read 1 Samuel 30. How did David handle the wind of discouragement that tried to distract his aim?

---

[1]   Idea from the free game archive, www.thesource4ym.com/GAMES/

- Compare an archer to a Christian. How are they alike? What things do they both have to remember?

COLLECT

Research the following scriptures: Song of Solomon 8:6-7, Isaiah 40:31, and Matthew 5:14-16.

Take the time to read these scriptures with your group. Share your insight. How will these verses help you get pass a dimly burning wick?

AFFECT

Remember your scripture partner. Congratulations! You have met your new prayer partner for this study. Take the time to get with your accountability partner at the end of each session. If comfortable, share a "dimly burning wick" request for your partner to help you pray about. Share about an area in your life that you desire to see grow and glow. If you are not able to share this yet, pray together for God to do amazing things in each other's lives through this Bible study.

There is a God shaped vacuum in the heart of every man which cannot be filled by any created thing, but only by God, the Creator, made known through Jesus.

Blaise Pascal

CHAPTER 2

A Knitted Frame

If I say something boldly, will you please love me anyway? Good! Here goes! Friend, God didn't knit just so you could sit! God didn't form you to be a space-taker but rather a difference-maker as a saltshaker to spread salt on this earth.

There is not a neutral gear when it comes to serving God. You are either moving forward with a fiery aim or moving backward. Shame, shame, shame! Your frame was absolutely knitted for activation, celebration, and illumination. Even before you were created, you were in the mind of God. I just bask in the thought that God had already planned every detail of my life before I took one breath on this earth.

In fact, before God ever formed us, He saw the big picture from beginning to end. Psalm 139:15 reminds us of that. "My frame was not hidden from you when I was made in the secret place. When I was woven together in the depths of the earth, your eyes saw my unformed body. All the days ordained for me were written in your book before one of them came to be."

Does your mind ever wonder what it was like when God spoke your name into existence in your mother's womb? Let's go further. Do you ever wonder what God might have said when He created you? I do. Sometimes, I try to guess what God might have said when He called out my name. Maybe something like, "Now, this one is going to love to rhyme . . . big time!" (Humor!)

But then I get serious and flip to the book of Genesis as I grab a hold of a new idea. In Genesis 1:3, when God created the world, His first thoughts and words were about light. "And God said, 'Let there be light,' and there was light." Hmm, that got me thinking. I just really wonder if, at that very moment God breathed His breath into your knitted frame, He was still thinking about brilliant light.

I like to imagine, as God watched you grow in your mother's womb, He whispered something like this over you, "Precious (insert your name), I love you with an everlasting love. I am forming you to be the light of the world" (Matt 5:14).

Now, you try. Tell me what you think God said when He designed your frame. Okay, I'll help you some more. I think He could have said something like this, "You will be a spark who will guide others to the ark. You will be a joyful flame that will deeply learn to praise My name." I like to believe that His thoughts were all about your luminescent light that He would use to lead others to Him.

The Bible reminds us over and over that, one day, we will give an account of our life on this Earth. I sure long to hear Him say when I meet Him face to face one day, "Flaming one, your light was good" (Gen 1:4).

You Were Created To Be a Fiery Design

Do you believe that God loves the fiery dreamer inside of you? Work with me here, and nod your head yes. God created you with so many gifts and abilities that specifically match His blazing passions for your frame. You titillate God's heart when you dream big! What a privilege it is to have the opportunity to dream deep and wide and watch our destiny collide with those God-given visions. It thrills me to pieces to know that God is the shaper despite negative reports on paper. God has a beautiful plan!

He has a specific intent, and He will not relent in spite of present circumstances. He wants our knitted frame to be a fiery flame just like Him. It doesn't take an Einstein to understand how our Divine likes things to shine. I want us to look at some fiery scriptures. Let's focus our lens on some tens.

In Daniel 10:6, the Bible tells us that Daniel saw a man with eyes like "flaming torches." In Daniel 7:9-10, Daniel tells us that God's throne "was flaming with fire and its wheels were all ablaze" and a "river of fire was flowing, coming out from before him." Are you seeing the fiery connection here?

In addition, Ezekiel saw "a figure like that of a man . . . full of fire, and that from there down he looked like fire; and brilliant light surrounded him" (Ezek 1:26-27). In Revelation, John describes someone "like a son of man" whose eyes were "like blazing fire" (Rev 1:13-14). When John shared his vision of the throne of God, he saw seven lamps that were "blazing" (Rev 4:5).

So here is my question for you. Based on the way you are living today, does the world see any fire exploding from your clay? Do people around you see your armor of light for Christ? Who is your blind Helen Keller sitting in a dark cellar in desperate need of your moving propeller of truth? According to gobiblestudy.com, Helen Keller certainly spoke with an arrow of truth when she said, "It is a terrible thing to see and have no vision." In Psalm 115:5, God addressed this thought also when He spoke of people who have eyes, "but they cannot see." My prayer is that God will give us eyes of blazing and radiant fire!

Speaking of radiance, let's head for the special man who got the radiant plan, Moses. Exodus 34:29 says, "When Moses came down from Mount Sinai with the two tablets of the Testimony in his hands, he was not aware that his face was radiant because he had spoken with the LORD." Moses's light didn't fizzle out because he chiseled out obedience, worship, fasting, and God's divine Word. When you are determined to have a quiet place with God and an open heart, people around you should see a beaming difference. The flaming fire inside of you is a sign of God's presence in your life. Genesis 15:17-21, Exodus 3, and 1 Kings 18:38-39 are just a few examples of how God's presence can change lives, attitudes, situations, and destinies.

As a knitted frame with the purpose to aim, God wants us to flame our best and leave the rest of every puzzling quest in His hands.

Ignore Satan's Stop Sign

As a daughter of the Most High, it breaks my heart that so many people have stopped their daily chase for more of God. The enemy has shoved a stop sign in their face and convinced them that God doesn't really want good things for them. Uh! Double uh! That is so far from the truth.

How many times have you heard someone say, "I guess it wasn't meant for me to be happy"? Go ahead and raise that hand in the air. Mine is already there. However, I'm ready to turn over a new leaf.

Will you partner with me in this new challenge? The next time we are tempted to start our sentence off with a downhearted, "I guess it wasn't meant . . ." we need to repent of that stinking scent. We need to focus our telescope on God's unending hope. We need to focus our blur to our flaming future (Jer 29:11).

Right now, your situation may have pinned you in a deep well or barred cell with no drive to propel. Lord, help this message to be as clear as a bell. If you really want your flame to aim blue, you have to say "so long" to the self-dependent you. You must tell self-sufficiency, "Good-bye." And on God you must rely. The Father has abundant blessings awaiting you. Don't stop short. Let Him escort you to the "great and unsearchable things" (Jer 33:3).

Light Is God's Headline

"Tonya, my life is such a mess! I think I was destined to live in the dark." Hold it! If that's your thought, do me a favor. Practice your archery skills right now. You see, every archer knows what important role the mind plays in reaching the target. The mind has control of all the muscles that allow your fingers to shoot the arrow successfully.

Likewise, your mind has control of how you shoot arrows of life or death with the power of your tongue. So put that word "dark" immediately in "park." Don't ever let it drive forward in your mind again. God didn't create you for darkness, my friend. There is absolutely no way God said, "Let there be darkness" when He created you. How do I know that? I've read it in His Word.

Darkness is not God's best because it is Satan's address (Matt 22:13). Because of the fall of man, we were born in sin, but we don't have to live there. When you repent of your sins and accept Christ as your Savior, the Word plainly says you "do not belong to the night or to the darkness" (1Thess 5:5). God has "called you out of darkness into his wonderful light" (1 Pet 2:9).

Just as arrows are used to kill from a great distance, we must use our spiritual arrows to eradicate any emotion or idea that doesn't come from Christ. Any thought that surrounds you with shade is not a thought that God has made. Take it captive immediately. Come to the mind of Christ and think "light" for your frame.

Psalm 104:2 says God "wraps Himself in light as with a garment." Like a butterfly in a chrysalis, God longs to wrap us into a new creature with God-filled ideas. You might feel like a moth in a dark place, but God knitted your frame to be a butterfly wrapped in the safety of His love and His light. "God is light; in him there is no darkness at all" (1 John 1:5). God wants to reveal Himself to you in a brand-new way.

Promise me this. No more anorexic faith from this moment on. Bind and grind those dead bones of faith. (You can't see me, but I'm pointing my finger at myself.) Even when it seems like a long delay, God is still working by His Plan A. You might be saying, "Tonya, you don't know my situation." You're right. I don't. But I know mine, and I'm going to shine a genuine faith in a God who works for me, not against me!

You Were Created to Be One of a Kind

I've told God more than once that I really don't want to be a normal worshipper. I just don't think I'm anointed to be normal! Can you tell? I see that head nodding! Actually, I don't think any of us are anointed to be normal. We were not designed to be a cookie-cutter worshipper. We were knitted to flame with origination. We need to quit looking around and start looking up. We need to quit looking at how everybody else does things and start asking God how He wants it done. We need to quit making excuses for why we don't want to cooperate with God when He wants to do a new thing and stretch us to a new place.

It doesn't matter what your past looks like. Today is a new day. Even if you weren't raised with godly training, you can't allow that to be an excuse. We must find our identity in Christ and be thrilled that He knitted us to be His instrument for something new. Then we can step out of the boat of comfort and do what God has put in our heart to do, even if it has never been done before. All the better. That's what Asa did.

Although Asa's father and mother had chosen sinful living, Asa flamed on to be one of Judah's most devout kings. Asa realized his distinctive place in the kingdom. And he got busy! As a result, Asa made a difference in worship as he "removed the foreign altars and the high places, smashed the sacred stones and cut down the Asherah poles" (2 Chron 14:3). We need to throw away the world's measuring stick and be determined to live out the exciting life God has planned for our frame.

Sunshine, you were created for vision and creativity before you ever took one breath. You must stop that negative critique because you are unique. The gifts that God has given to you are distinctive. No one can take your place in fulfilling your dreams.

God wants your fire to snap, crackle, and pop to reach a huge crop of unbelievers. And He has given you everything to do just that. I earnestly pray you will become more aware that were created to "let your light shine before men, that they may see your good deeds and praise your Father in heaven" (Matt 5:16).

TRUSTING CHRIST MUST BE YOUR LIFE'S OUTLINE

I just love reading about Job. You have to admit that his arrow wouldn't quit. His aim was toward God. Though trials tried to distract his bow and arrow away from the target of loyalty, Job stood his ground. This man outlined his life with a powerful word called trust. In Job 1-2, we see an archer who trusted God's sovereignty.

Take note. Job's speech wasn't slurred. His vision wasn't blurred. His mouth continually concurred that God was worthy of praise in spite of his pain. Because Job concurred, Satan never said another word in the next forty chapters. The accuser was the loser. Job drank the purposed cup that shut up the devil. Whoo! I like that! That is what trust in Christ will do for you.

We are so mistaken if we ever think the enemy is going to leave us alone. I can assure you that Satan has a destructive aim heading right toward your flame. According to Job 6:4, we can conclude that arrows of the enemy used in fighting during Job's time were often dipped in poison. And so it is with the enemy. Today, Satan shoots out poisoned arrows with the intent to kill your zeal for Christ.

One way Satan tries to steal your zeal is through a cup of suffering. He knows a cup of suffering will open up a temptation to gag your praise and zigzag your blaze for Christ. If permitted, Satan will use any nag to trash bag your kingdom purposes. However, when you choose to take aim and flame, you can't back up. You drink that cup while looking up. And God will reward you more than you could ever imagine.

Speaking of the words "more than," have you ever seen a mother play the "more than that" game with her child? It is the cutest thing. The child stretches out those innocent arms real big and asks, "Mommy, do you love me this much?" The parent responds, "More than that!" The child stretches those arms a little wider and asks the same question again, "Mommy, do you love me this much?" The parent responds again, "More than that!" However, this time, the parent adds a great big, unsuspected tickle, right under those little outstretched arms. The child is left with a squirm of joy.

Through the years of trials, I have been that squirmy little one who stretched out her arms in desperation. "Father, do you love me this much? Am I really, really valuable to you?" And He responds, "More than many sparrows" (Matt 10:31). "Father, am I really a conqueror who can make it through this trial?" And he responds, "You are more than a conqueror through Me" (Rom 8:37). "Father, do you really have great things in store for me?" And He responds again, "More than all you could ask or imagine" (Eph 3:20).

If your bow and arrow will continue to remain firm, you'll always experience the joy in the squirm. Tender one, I know it often seems that God's ways are strange, but they are always long range. He has a higher goal. Your job is to behold Him. Keep the eyes of your face fixed on His grace.

He has already declared an end to that restrain and pain. In Isaiah 46:10, God said, "I make known the end from the beginning, from ancient times, what is still to come. I say: My purpose will stand, and I will do all that I please." He has a purpose in the pain and blessings to gain if we will stay put, wipe off the soot, and focus on God's input in everything we do.

KEEPING GOD'S LOVE ON YOUR MIND

Here's something good to remember. If you allow your flesh to rule, your flame is going to cool. The fact of science is that a flame will cool as it moves away from the source of the heat. And so it is with us. We must stay the course and be connected to the source, Jesus Christ. We must be drawn to keep God's love on our minds daily. We must repeatedly tell ourselves how much Christ loves us if we are going to sustain through the strain of life's challenges.

God's Word encourages us to love Him with all that is within us because that love will sustain through the hard times. I pray right now that you will cultivate a love that "always protects, always trusts, always hopes, always perseveres" (1 Cor 13:7).

There is absolutely no limit to what God can do with a frame that falls in love with Him. Need validation? Flip back to 1 Corinthians 2:9 as it reads, "No eye has seen, no ear has heard, no mind has conceived what God has prepared for those who love him." Who what? Love Him!

You can't allow your trials to tame your flame. When Satan tries to extinguish it, you must relinquish it (trust) to your Abba Father. What you direct, God will protect. Satan will use trials to weigh down your faith and love for Christ. Get rid of the weight as you turn to Matthew 11:28. "Come to me, all you who are weary and burdened, and I will give you rest."

No matter where you are in life, you're always ripe for a setback. Defeat begins with one thought to hold back on Jesus. One thought to quit. One thought to doubt that God would ever give you those great desires. Satan will try to get you to tame your flame by pulling back on the rein. If the enemy can use a circumstance to cool you down from your fiery devotion to the Father, he has a foothold. If Satan can get you to wane, he is one step closer to your flame. If you become lax, you will wax away. From this day on, I want you to believe that God can use you for another one's breakthrough. Our Lord can use anything you have been through to flame for Him.

The goal of every believer should come alive every time he reads John 5:35. We should all desire for God to see in us what He saw in His beloved disciple, "a lamp that burned and gave light." Precious child of purpose, a holy name framed you to be a holy flame. God wants to inflame your fire with His desire so you will inspire others.

According to englishforums.com, Dante Alighieri, an Italian poet, once said, "From a little spark may burst a mighty flame." I can't tell you how many times I have wanted to give up on God's visions for my life. Then God would spark my heart with the thought, "Come on, little blue. I'm counting on you!"

May you be drawn to remember that your loving Savior stepped into your dark so you could be a spark for Him. As you journey through this book, I hope you laugh. I hope you cry. I hope you ball up that fist and scream out, "Yes! I choose to take aim and flame!"

BIBLE STUDY IDEAS

CONNECT

This is going to be fun for all of you who can't sing. Break up into small groups. Your group leader will assign you a character's name that God knitted for a special assignment. When your group gets the Bible character's name, you must write a song describing the character's special task and how he or she completed the work. Do not include the character's name in the song because the other groups will be asked to guess who your "knitted frame" is. Here's the kicker. The song needs to be to the tune of a children's song. Here are a few suggestions: "Mary Had a Little Lamb" or "Itsy Bitsy Spider." Be creative. Make it fun and hilarious! Sing pretty now!

DIRECT

Share with your group a highlighted thought that ministered to you.

REFLECT

- In this chapter, we discussed many scriptures that connected God with fire. Research some examples in the Bible where God used fire to symbolize His presence or judgment. What can we learn from these?
- Just as fire is used to purify metal, God can use difficult situations to purify our hearts. Read Matthew 5:8 and Psalm 24:3-5. What are the benefits of a pure heart?
- You are a knitted frame. What are some of your knitted gifts that God has given you to build up the body of Christ?
- Many times, we struggle with new assignments that God gives to our knitted frame. What are some of the assignments that you feel God is stretching you to do?
- Can you think of any characters in the Bible who had a self-sacrificing passion to minister light in a dark situation? How did his or her passion change the situation? How should that inspire us?
- Read Jeremiah 1. Notice some of the things that God said to Jeremiah. How can those same words encourage us to fulfill our calling?

Collect

Research the following scriptures: Jeremiah 1:5, Isaiah 42:6, Isaiah 61:1-3, and Mark 16:15. Take the time to read these with your group. Share your insight. How will these scriptures help you focus on being a knitted frame designed to flame?

Affect

Take the time to get with your accountability partner. Pray for your partner's gifts and strengths to be saturated with a feverish passion. Pray for enthusiasm to fulfill the call for your knitted frames. Pray that God will show your partner the "unsearchable things" that He promised in Jeremiah 33:3.

When you become consumed by God's call on your life, everything will take on new meaning and significance. You will begin to see every facet of your life—including your pain—as a means through which God can work to bring others to Himself.

Charles Stanley

CHAPTER 3

I Know My Name

One of the saddest news reports I have ever watched on television was about the shooter in the Virginia Tech massacre, Seung-Hui Cho. It was reported this young man, created in God's own image, would sign his name in college with a question mark.[2] It has been many years since this incident happened. However, I still cry when I think about the pain for the family and friends of the victims, as well as the pain for Seung-Hui Cho's family.

A question mark. I just can't get away from those three words. How different things would have turned out if this young man had understood that his name had a purpose to aim and flame for Christ. I wish I could have sat beside him in class. He might have thought I was a pest, but I would have spilled out my unstoppable zest to remind him of his name, Loved.

We encounter so many people who that question mark enslaves. As a flame, we must run to them and share, "You don't have to be enslaved. Your name is engraved in the palms of God's hands" (Isa 49:16).

I don't want you to end this chapter until you realize that a question mark can never fill the space of your name. May you become more enthralled with the thought that your name is Loved.

---

[2]   FOX NEWS.com, "Virginia Tech Gunman Raised Concerns With Disturbing Writing," http://www.foxnews.com/story/0,2933,266582,00.html.

Love Is Your Bookmark

It was easy to accept the thought that my name was Loved when I could eat what I wanted and walk wherever I wanted to. However, that season of suffering came when I could do neither. I'll never forget the moment I looked in the mirror and saw this ninety-pound speaker and writer sitting in a wheelchair. I didn't feel so loved. I felt more shoved. "God, why am I here? This is not what you've shown me! You have forgotten about me! You have abandoned me!" I cried.

Oh, yeah! I really thought that more than once. Come on, now. We are friends, and I can be perfectly honest with you, right? I realize now that the old, sneaky question mark was trying to make its way into my life and take the place of my name, Loved. I felt so lost in the chapters of my life.

With tears streaming down my face, I did it. I rolled my wheelchair up close to the mirror and decided I was through with my pity party. I pointed my bony finger in the mirror and cried, "Tonya Bennett, God loves you, and He has good plans for you! Nothing can separate you from the love of God" (Rom 8:38).

Can I be real? I don't even know if I really believed what I said at that time, but something supernatural happened to me. Somewhere, in the midst of it all, I began to feel deeply drawn to take aim and flame. The depth of God's love began to swell up inside me. I felt the love of the Father, Son, and Holy Spirit in the most unique way. I felt an ignited spark pushing against my question mark. At that very second, love truly became my bookmark. It was the ribbon that marked my place in staying committed to this frustrated race. God's amazing, personal, deep-felt love became my anchor to what felt like just lost pages of my destiny. Overwhelmingly, I felt the drip of God's love.

God is searching for some loyal and committed people who He can equip to stay focused on the drip of His constant love. Are you tempted to jump ship? Focus on the drip. Facing a hardship? Focus on the drip. Has your passion lost its skip? Focus on the drip. Made a slip? Focus on the drip of God's everlasting love showering down on you and drawing you back into fellowship with Him.

I just get all excited every time I read John 17:23 where it says that God loves us just like He loves Christ. It blows my mind how God's love is that defined. Precious one, don't allow any room in your brain for a question mark to remain. Fill your mind with the love of Christ. From that moment forward, I didn't feel the same. I felt the calling of my new name, Mrs. Flame. I felt the heart of a flaming warrior.

In the Old Testament, the Hebrew word for warrior is "gibbor," which refers to one who has strength that surpasses ordinary strength. Like Gideon, God is calling you to be a "mighty warrior" (Jgs 6:12).

Throughout the Bible, God gave many people new names that were symbols of how He had changed them. I'm convinced that my new name changed the moment I realized that, in spite of and despite of my confusing circumstances, "an everlasting love" treasured me (Jer 31:3). I am convinced that God can bring deep triumph from any trial with His overwhelming love.

In fact, I think that's how David must have felt in Psalm 42:7-8 when he said, "Deep calls to deep, in the roar of your waterfalls; all your waves and breakers have swept over me. By day the Lord directs his love, at night his song is with me—a prayer to the God of my life."

David was facing his own question mark, but His revelation of God's love drew Him to a place where he was determined to take aim and flame. Even through the roar, he learned to soar above the storms with a confident heart in Christ.

Sometimes, I just love to place my head on the armrest of our recliner and imagine my head in the lap of God. As Abba Father strengthens my spirit man and catches every tear that falls from my eyes, He reminds me to keep myself in His love while I wait upon Him (Jude 1:21).

God has given me a new passion to find those question marks all around me and bookmark them with encouragement. All I want to do is grab a hold of a weary soldier's hand and help him learn to take a stand against that destructive plan of a question mark.

REMOVING THE QUESTION MARK

We don't like to think this way, but in reality, souls have question marks. Identities have question marks. Marriages have questions marks. Ministries have questions marks. Parenting has question marks. Questions marks pack hospitals. School systems have question marks. The government has question marks. The economy has question marks. How about you? Are you sitting in the dark with a question mark?

Friend, you may be reading this book, and you are such a good person. You work hard. You love your family. You are a sweet spouse or parent. You have morals. You treat others with sincere kindness. You put your whole heart into your work, and you do it with enthusiasm. However, you have not personally asked Jesus to come into your heart and forgive you of all your sins. Just being a good person won't get your name in the Lamb's Book of Life.

Tenderly, I want to share with you the most important sentence in this book. God longs for you to know your name as not only loved but also forgiven. However, in order to know your name is forgiven, you have to know the only "name under heaven given to men by which we must be saved" (Acts 4:12). Anyone who has never personally asked Jesus Christ to forgive him or her of his or her sins has allowed the question mark to take the place of his or her name.

Many people say, "Oh, yeah, I believe in God." Well, that's a start. However, we must remember that "even the demons believe that—and shudder" (James 2:19). God desires that we know the name of Jesus personally and intimately. God yearns for us to "believe that Jesus is the Christ, the Son of God, and that by believing you may have life in his name" (John 20:31).

Those who don't choose to believe and follow Christ are in the dark. On Judgment Day, they will stand before the Lord with a question mark. Romans 1:20 is very clear. No excuse will be accepted for that question mark.

For so many, the message in this book may taste sour, but to others, they will taste power. "For the message of the cross is foolishness to those who are perishing, but to us who are being saved it is the power of God" (1 Cor 1:18).

Satan is a liar, and he is after your holy fire. He wants to eliminate your spark with a question mark. He knows that question marks will hold back and hold out on God. Question marks will miss their story for God's glory. Question marks will live life in the haze and never be a blaze for their Maker. They will never allow their wax to overflow to the max. They will live out there on lust and never fully trust in the benefits of living God's way. Question marks will never drip with an anointed scent and beautifully imprint the lives of others.

So just how does Satan get us to fall for the question mark? Think about it this way. Whenever you see a period at the end of a sentence, do you know what it means? Done. Closure. Finished.

When Jesus died on the cross, He said, "It is finished." Settled. Mission accomplished. No other sacrifice would ever be needed for His people. The key to death, hell, and the grave belongs to Christ. Period.

The scheme of Satan seems to be to attach a comma over the period. Satan loves a comma. A pause. A delay. A space. A wait time. Satan uses a comma to camouflage a question mark. Satan often whispers, "Why do you have to accept Jesus as your Savior now? It's more fun to thrive in sin than to live a holy life all caved in. You can't have fun living by the Bible. Come on. Buy my line. You have plenty of time. Take the comma. Wait a little longer. Have some fun. Live life to the fullest your way. Come on, man. This is a cool plan. Live like you want to. After all, you only get one chance to live it up." Satan very well knows that a comma will result in one becoming more and more entangled in sin.

How many people has Satan convinced that a period results in a boring life instead of a soaring life? Dear one, if you choose to put your desires over God's desires, you have just placed a comma over God's period. As a result, you have pushed aside the flame and formed a question mark in place of your name. You have selected cursing over blessing. Hell instead of heaven.

Friend, I'm not giving you an opinion, I'm sharing the Word. Revelation 20:15 says, "If anyone's name was not found written in the book of life, he was thrown into the lake of fire."

One of God's greatest gifts to us is free will. It's your choice. Jesus won't force you to repent and become a new creature in Christ. He has a flame pictured by your name. But if you fail to choose Christ, you'll never set aim. On Judgment Day, you will be responsible for your shame because you rejected His wonderful name.

ARE YOU READY TO LEAVE A MARK?

Don't forget this now. As a mouse is drawn to cheese, so the devil is drawn to the keys of your future. Satan wants you handcuffed to sin and bound from within. He will eavesdrop until He finds a way to swap the truth for a lie. Why? Satan wants you separated and alienated from the source of light. He loves for your life to be filled with noisy racket and a question mark packet so you will not mature in Christ. The enemy doesn't want you in church doing a soul search of how you can become more effective for Christ. He doesn't want your aim hard-core and unable to trip you up with those same things anymore.

Your enemy would much rather you settle for the question mark than experience a new birth. Why? Satan knows his lease is about to cease on earth. Jesus is coming soon. Therefore, every name should make it his aim to be a moon, a light that reflects the Son. The only thing that can keep you from being a reflection is your own rejection to the light. God longs to help us keep our lives free from a question mark.

When the imps of hell come around to tease or freeze my purpose for existence, I shout, "I am a frame that knows her name. It's Mrs. Flame." You see, if you're going to leave a mark in this life, you have to know who you are in Christ. You are not a misfit. Your candle has been lit to become a smash hit for Christ. One day, your smash hit will see Satan thrown into the bottomless pit. Doesn't that thought just send you straight to your feet with a "Hallelujah" holler?

When you feel like just a smoking ember, take the time to remember, "While we were still sinners, Christ died for us" (Rom 5:8).

If we are going to leave a mark in our heritage, we must also know that our name is forgiven. That means we can cast any hurtful past on the one who can full blast our sins "as far as the east is from the west" (Ps 103:12). Every time I read Isaiah 62:2, I can't help but to yell, "Yahoo!" I love the part that says, "You will be called by a new name that the mouth of the LORD will bestow. You will be a crown of splendor in the LORD's hand, a royal diadem in the hand of your God."

Like Abraham, God has made your name to be a blessing (Gen 12:2). I am a frame who knows her name because my sins "have been forgiven on account of his name" (1 John 2:12). My flame can't help but to glow because I know "everyone whose name is found written in the book—will be delivered" (Dan 12:1).

Satan targets your flame to remove the name of Jesus from being your priority. He knows that "to those who believed in his name, he gave the right to become children of God" (John 1:12). He is doing his best to remove the mark of Christ's name from everything.

Who do you think has stirred the holler to get God off the dollar? Who do you think has stirred the fuss to get Christ out of Christmas? Who do you think played it cool to get prayer taken out of school? Satan has enslaved and raved because he knows "everyone who calls on the name of the Lord will be saved" (Rom 10:13).

No matter what others might say, the name of Jesus Christ is the only way. If you are feeling a tug on that question mark, I pray you will not delay to know "the way and the truth and the life" (John 14:6). If you are the one who God designed this chapter for, don't wait another minute. I pray you will place this book down, say, "That's me," and ABC right there on your knee. *Ask* Him in. *Believe* from within. *Confess* your sin.

Romans 10:9 says, "That if you confess with your mouth, 'Jesus is Lord,' and believe in your heart that God raised him from the dead, you will be saved." If you have already accepted Jesus as your Savior, please take a few moments to stop and pray for those who have not committed their lives to Christ. Rather, they have accepted the question mark in place of their name. The most important decision one will ever make is to join the family tree of the land of the free.

GETTING READY FOR A NEW SPARK

Once you've joined the heavenly choir, you can get ready for the passionate fire. You see, when blood is applied, fire is not denied. God has always specified this order: blood first and then fire will burst. Elijah knew the sequence. He applied wood, and then he stood to see what God could and would do with his obedience.

God is always drawn to the burning scent when a child of purpose chooses to repent. When one gives his heart to Christ, he is made new. "Therefore, if anyone is in Christ, he is a new creation; the old has gone, the new has come" (2 Cor 5:17).

As you hunger for God's Word and intimacy with your Savior, you will see your decisions and desires move in a new direction. You will no longer be content with being a blender to the world's corruptive desires. You will crave to surrender to the tender leading of the Holy Spirit. The fingers of God formed your name to be set apart for His glory. "Before I formed you in the womb, I knew you, before you were born I set you apart; I appointed you as a prophet to the nations" (Jer 1:5).

Jesus has always had our name attached to "do good works, which God prepared in advance for us to do" (Eph 2:10). When you truly understand your existence, you will go the distance with persistence to fight every resistance. Isn't that what a candle does? When a sparkling candle enters the room, there's no debate. Light carries the most weight. The light of a flame wins every time. Hands down! Come to think of it. Even the shape of a candle's wick reminds me of an exclamation mark. Lord, may our heart's desire be to flame with excitement!

Flaming one, there is so much more God has in store if you will open the door and just let Him pour. Then He will make you a mentor for a brother's trapdoor. Who in your family is about to give up right now and needs your flame to guide him somehow? Who is sitting in the dark needing you to share with him how to embark on a new fulfilling life? I just love to read testimonies of people who refuse to settle for the dark. Instead, they chose to be a flame.

Jabez Refused to Settle for the Dark

Will you join me as we open the door to a precious mentor found in 1 Chronicles 4? In this chapter, you trot along this long list of names until . . . boom! A great potential for doom who chose to trade his tomb for a sonic boom interrupted you. One who pushed for the best and got his request. That would be Jabez.

His mother might have pushed with great pain, but Jabez pushed to get great gain. He refused the dark. He pushed away the question mark. He must have said, "My name is not pain. My name is Mr. Flame." This fellow wouldn't settle for a name that meant sorrow. Like Jabez, we must get past the opinions of man and push toward all that God has designed for our name.

First, Jabez pushed toward a dream. He understood that he had been planned for grand. Like a rubber band, he was asking God to stretch him to new places and spaces. When you tap into God's purpose for your life, nothing can hold you back. You can't dream too big because God owns the whole oil rig. When He anoints you with His oil to do it, He will walk you all the way through it. Then your passion to fulfill His desires will drive you until you reach breakthrough.

Second, not only did Jabez have a dream, he focused on the Supreme. Jabez was confident that God was able to fulfill all He was asking. When God fires up your ignition with a specific mission, you become driven. When your dream is attached to the harvest, get ready! God likes to fertilize what He has organized and will leave you quite surprised at the results.

Jabez knew he would get the thoughts that "outnumber the grains of sand" when he got the hand of God (Ps 139:18). We need to ask for God's hand on everything we do. When the Supreme guides your candle, it can't help but to beam.

Many people don't know their name because they keep focusing on their shame. Every time the enemy calls you defeated and depleted, don't ever hang around to argue. Just simply nod that head while focusing on your red (target) and say, "That's my name!"

God calls me His child (John 1:12). God calls me His friend (John 15:15). God calls me justified through faith (Rom 5:1). God calls me free from condemnation (Rom 8:1). God calls me redeemed (Col 1:13). God calls me anointed (2 Cor 1:21). God calls me His workmanship (Eph 2:10). God calls me a child of light (Eph 5:8).

Be aware. Satan will always try to sell you death insurance. He wants you to sign your name to his dotted, spotted, rotted, and knotted line of destruction. We must push aside the pen with a glorious grin and shout, "Take your pen back because I've got spiritual AFLAC insurance. I am accepted, forgiven, loved, anointed, and committed to Christ."

Before we close this chapter, I want us to look at some people in the Bible whose names were never mentioned, yet they played an important part in teaching us how to take aim and flame. We may not feel like the world knows our name, but God does, and He knows exactly how He will use us to be a flame.

1. **Judges 9:50-57: Woman of Thebez.** Abimelech wanted power. He killed many people yet he met his match when he went to a place called Thebez. As he approached a tower, he was not prepared for a woman to push a millstone onto his head. He commanded his armor bearer to kill him because he couldn't bear the thought of a woman defeating him. Just like this woman, we must carry a light to fight against the enemy of our soul. We might not know this woman's biblical name, but her spiritual name was Ms. Flame.

2. **2 Kings 5:1-14: Maid of Naaman's Wife.** Like many of us, Naaman fell for the prideful game, but that wouldn't stop

his servant's flame. Elisha's messenger had told Naaman, a man of leprosy, to go and wash seven times in the Jordan River and he would be healed. Although the prideful flick was affecting Naaman's wick, the maid kept fanning his flame with encouragement. As a result, Naaman obeyed the word of the prophet and was made whole. We are never given the servant's name, but we can surely praise God for her purpose to flame and nudge a man to receive his healing. Our greatest mission in life should be a squealer that nudges another name to the Healer.

3. **Matthew 9:20-22, Mark 5:25-34, and Luke 8: 43-48: Woman with Issue of Blood.** We don't know her name or the amount of her tears, but we do know this woman suffered for twelve long years. For so long, her life must have felt like a disaster, but it quickly changed when she touched the Master. This woman leaves us with a beautiful example of a flamer who pushed past the crowd to get her healing.

May I encourage you to be a flame who knows his or her name and "do not be ashamed, but praise God that you bear that name" (1 Pet 4:16). Our world is facing a desperate condition with a devilish demolition in families, marriages, self-esteem, ministries, finances, and so forth. We don't have to get caught in the onslaught of a question mark. We can know our name is Flame!

BIBLE STUDY IDEAS

CONNECT[3]
The group leader should have already thought of names for the following categories: Bible names, Bible animals, and Bible places. If you have eighteen people, you would have thought of nine names, nine animals, and nine places. Each person will tape a sign on his or her back with one of these categories. His or her job is to try to find out who he or she is. You can only ask "yes or no" questions.

---

[3]   Idea from the free game archive, www.TheSource 4YM.com

DIRECT

Share with your group a highlighted thought that ministers to you.

REFLECT

- How does the name you accept over your life affect your daily choices?
- Think back over this past year. Which name of God has been the most personal to you?
- Research the following names: Adonai, El Roi, Jehovah-Jireh, Jehovah-Shalom, Jehovah-Rapha, El Elyon, Elohim, El Roi, El Shaddai, Jehovah M'Kaddesh, Jehovah Nissi, Jehovah Rohi, Jehovah Sabaoth, Jehovah Shalom, Jehoavah Shammah, and Jehovah Tsidkenu. Think back over this past week. Which name has been the most personal to you?
- This week, challenge yourself to begin praising Jesus for who is. Get yourself acquainted with His name. Let's practice right now. As a group, begin calling out names from the letter A to Z of who Jesus is to you. Example: Jesus is A: Almighty, Jesus is B: Bread of Life, C: Jesus is my Comforter. (Little help on letter X: Jesus is Excellent. That will work.) As you are riding in the car or simply doing house chores, begin to praise God for who He is by simply using the alphabet. Oh, how blessed Our Father will be.
- What name has Jesus revealed to you about who you are to Him that has made a shift in your thinking?
- Have the group brainstorm different names of different types of candy. The group leader can already have some suggested candies posted. Ask each person to select two names of candy that would best describe the process God has done in your life. Pick one name that describes you in the past and one name that describes a change in your life. Here are some suggested choices: Zero, Kisses, Lifesavers, Snickers, Bit of Honey, Whatchamacallit, Mr. Goodbar, Almond Joy, Ice Breaker, Hershey's Bliss, Turtles, Maple Nut Goodies, Jelly Beans, Saltwater Taffy, Treasure Butter Toffee, and Diamond Almonds. Explain. At one time, I felt like a _____ because . . . Now I am more of a _____ because . . .

COLLECT

Research the following scriptures that share the names of the Holy Spirit: Isaiah 11:2, John 14:16-26, Romans 1:4, Ephesians 1:17, and Hebrews 10:29. Take the time to read these with your group. Share your insight. How does the Holy Spirit help us to flame on?

AFFECT

Which one of the names of God do you need ministering to right now? Do you need His provision or peace in some area? Share with your partner this need. Pray for each other that God will be so personal in that specific area.

As Christians, I challenge you. Have a great aim—have a high standard—make Jesus your ideal . . . make Him an ideal not merely to be admired but also to be followed.

Eric Liddell

─── CHAPTER 4 ────────────────────────

Take Aim

According to Merriam-Webster, one definition of the word "aim" is to "direct toward a specific object or goal." When one accepts Christ as His Savior, he must keep a tight grip on his spiritual bow and arrow. Even when faced with regret, an upset, lots of debt, or the "why not yet" questions, one must keep his eyes pointing in the direction of full commitment to the Father.

Jesus didn't halfway take our stripes or halfway carry our cross. His light was about our soul fight. And Jesus went all the way. Therefore, as Paul stated in his closing words to the Corinthians, we must "aim for perfection" (2 Cor 13:11). Just as a key component of archery shooting is consistency, we must also keep in mind how we can move toward a life of full obedience to Christ.

HAVE YOU CHOSEN TO STRADDLE?

Let's get a little exercise going here. Stand up and separate your feet. Little wider. Now say, "The battle is in the straddle." Dear one, might there be a fence you are trying to straddle? Have you chosen to place one leg in the church and one leg in the world?

I have personally learned this one well. The enemy will win if you ever teeter-totter about sin. If you side with the straddle, you'll settle to skedaddle down the wrong path. Your "up and down" will never get you on solid ground.

So let's go ahead and reflect. Is there anything in your life right now that you feel uneasy about? A person you haven't forgiven? A desire that you know hinders your spiritual growth? Oh, it's there. In fact, that area that you have tried to push back as far as you can is probably popping right up in your mind right now. Good, I want it to.

Now, don't start squirming because God is affirming that He wants to help you in that area. More and more, I am asking God to take every thought and action that displeases Him out of my life. Guess what? I am praying God does the same for you. I pray God has His finger right smack on that attack.

At all times, God's Word must be our target. With most targets I've seen, you aim for the red. Red is the key to victory. And so it is spiritually. We must aim for the R-E-D.

AIM FOR THE RED

RIGHTEOUSNESS
Noah was a man with an aim. Genesis 6:9 says, "Noah was a righteous man, blameless among the people of his time, and he walked with God." Noah was not a man without sin, but he was a flame who loved God wholeheartedly. When God spoke, Noah did not revoke. He fanned his flame and set his aim toward building a boat the length of one and a half football fields. Whoa, buddy! That would be tough on any rotator cuff.

I just love what the Lord said to Noah in Genesis 7:1, "Go into the ark, you and your whole family, because I have found you righteous in this generation." Can God say that about you? Consider the position of a candle, a light that stands upright. Are you influencing this generation by your aim for standing upright and obedient unto a holy God?

Like Jesus, Noah chose the hammer, despite the clamor of the world. If you truly desire to be a lampstand, you will also choose the hammer. According to Exodus 25:31, the lampstands were made of pure gold and had to be . . . oh, brace yourself . . . hammered out. It had to endure pounding and astounding strikes. Those things we struggle with have to be hammered out until we are enamored with God's desires. If we are going to have extraordinary beauty like the lampstands, we must also go through fire and be hammered until we are "of one piece" with God (Exod 25:36). Then every lampstand's purpose will be to "light the space in front of it" (Exod 25:37).

The enemy does not want your candle lit with the benefit of living righteous. So I am going to make a point to tell you how striving to live righteously can affect your life. Here are just a few:

1. God rewards the righteous (1 Sam 26:23).
2. God helps the righteous grow stronger (Job 17:9).
3. God blesses the righteous (Ps 5:12).
4. God sees and hears the cry of the righteous (Ps 34:15)
5. God delivers the righteous from their troubles (Ps 34:19).
6. God never forsakes them (Ps 37:25).
7. God makes them flourish (Ps 72:7).
8. God sheds His light on them (Ps 97:11).
9. God causes the lips of the righteous to nourish many (Prov 10:21).
10. God will cause the righteous to stand firm (Prov 10:25).
11. God rescues the righteous from trouble (Prov 11:8).
12. God will order the steps of the righteous (Ps 37:23).
13. God surrounds the righteous with His favor (Ps 5:12).

When living upright before the Lord is your pursuit, you will bear some irresistible fruit. Do you agree that, if we will aim and flame, our light has to produce fruit? Ephesians 5:9 says, "The fruit of the light consists in all goodness, righteousness and truth."

Our target must be toward the narrow gate. Satan doesn't fight with a chocolate-covered arrow. According to Ephesians 6:16, Satan fights with "flaming arrows." He will use things like your job, finances, marriage, sickness, fear, lustful desires, addictions, unequally yoked relationships, hurtful situations, bitterness, lack of confidence, and low self-esteem. But that's not his target. Satan uses all these to annoy, but his target is your joy because that's your life's buoy. The joy of the Lord keeps you from going down.

If we learn to aim right, we will be a radiant light. Then God "will make your righteousness shine like the dawn" (Ps 37:6).

Speaking of lights, that brings me to the next target.

EXCELLENCE

Do you have a minute for me to tell you about my plight with a light? Every December, I look so forward to decorating my Christmas tree with my family. But honestly, I have to admit that hanging the lights is not my strength. Not at all. Just ask my girls. My Christmas tree lights never cooperate with me. I don't know. I just fight with those lights. They twist and tangle from every single angle.

Finally, I pass the rattle of the light battle. The tree is all beautifully adorned with lots of laughs and cute little crafts. My girls and I raise the star and step back from afar to gaze and say, "Oh, what a tree of excellence." Then it happens. One little light starts blinking, and out it goes. I shout at the tree, "Oh, no, you are going to mess up my tree of excellence, Mr. Light." I shake and shake the cord, thinking that will make a difference. But it never does. My tree of excellence has lost its effervescence because of one little area.

Hang tight. I'm going somewhere here. What area is your barrier to producing light? Learn from me. The whole link will lose its blink. Attention, all readers, the thinking affects the blinking of your tree. If we have stinking thinking, we'll have shrinking blinking. That is why we need to aim for a spirit of excellence, just like one of my favorite characters, Daniel. This archer's mind was made up. Daniel knew a compromise would paralyze his effectiveness. He was not going to do anything that defiled his conscience. The Babylonians had set aim to change Daniel's thinking. However, this man had deep convictions that were not negotiable.

What about you? Are your convictions negotiable? How deep do your convictions lie? How much of the flesh do you crucify? Have you been made new in the attitude of your mind, like we are told in Ephesians 4:23? God has revealed to us what will cause shrinking blinking in Romans 1:21, "But their thinking became futile and their foolish hearts were darkened." There's no light when your thinking isn't right.

If you want to shine, you'd better know where to draw the line. No one is exempted from being tempted. We must decide ahead of time what choices will cause that grime. If I want to be a flame that gives glory to His name, I must strive for a spirit of excellence. The enemy is always setting traps of "cheese to please" the flesh. That is why we must guard our thinking. Remember this, sin can't mar whatever you guard.

As a nation, we have become slack and fell through the crack because we haven't attacked the lax spirit. The downward spiral of decaying morality doesn't seem to bother many Christians. We have allowed it to lurch right on into the church. We have entertained sin and let it come on in. It doesn't even have to ring the doorbell anymore. We don't even blush about the sudden rush of sin. Your target of excellence must always have a message for the enemy. It's very simple. "Sin is not getting in my temple!"

Hear me now because this is good. The very moment you are tempted to take a bite into something not right, you have to know how to fight. If you want to hit the bull's-eye, you must cry out to God immediately, "God, this is bigger than me, so I cast it on Thee!" You absolutely have to acknowledge your weakness before the Lord at the onset of temptation. Don't you dare chew, or it will brew. If you chew, you're through. I'm just saying.

Satan will subdue the true view of your target. We miss it when we think we are strong enough to handle things on our own strength and fail to cry out for help. If I had to pick one sentence that I want the angels to say about how I handle temptations, it would be, "Jesus, here comes little blue, crying out again for you." God, please help us to push pass "feel" to stay in the "will" of God.

I learned a long time ago that I can't handle temptations on my own. So I believe that crying out catapults you into developing a spirit of excellence. When you learn to aim for the spirit of excellence, you release a piece of control that is trying to trap you into living for yourself. We must continually admit how dependent we are on God's strength. Like a magnet, our Lord is drawn to humility!

Satan wants us to be like cows chewing cud when it comes to sin. He wants us to chew on temptations, swallow, and bring it back up again. Chew some more, swallow, and bring it back up in our minds again. Satan will rob us of God's best for our future by tempting us to chew and act upon those temptations. Satan knows that sin will disconnect us from God. We are reminded in Isaiah 59:2, "But your iniquities have separated you from God."

Like Daniel, we must resolve not to defile ourselves with the craving and enslaving of the twenty-first century. Daniel did not give into the vulture of his culture. He absolutely and resolutely refused to dishonor God.

The battleground is all about your loyalty. Your spirit of excellence must pledge loyalty to Christ in every course of action. How does God show up to a scene of loyalty? 2 Chronicles 16:9 says that God strengthens those "whose hearts are fully committed to him." May the Lord help us maintain a flame of steadfast allegiance to Him.

DISTINCTION

I am learning that a person whose flame will aim at distinction is a protector of convictions, restrictions, conflictions, and contradictions. If your feelings say, "Go! Go!" but the Word says, "No! No!" your aim to flame with distinction needs to step up to the plate and scream, "God's Word is my standard!"

Can we really build such strong convictions in our children that, generation after generation, our heritage will choose to say no? Like a wart on a frog, I'm sticking to this answer. Yes, you can!

Just ask Jonadab. He had such a zeal that was for real. In Jeremiah 35:14, God commends the family of Jonadab for keeping a particular aim. The Bible specifically shares with us how Jonadab chose to teach his family to refrain from participating in certain convictions for their heritage. Two hundred years later, legacies of commitment to their family's convictions were being passed down from generation to generation. Like arrows, we need to shape and sharpen our children to convictions that align with the Word. Psalm 127:4 says, "Like arrows in the hands of a warrior are sons born in one's youth."

Every person has to work out his own salvation "with fear and trembling" (Phil 2:12). But you can believe one thing. I search God's Word and find everything that our Bible magnifies, warns us against, and tells us will not inherit the kingdom of heaven, and I put it at the top of my parenting list of things to teach my children to refrain from participating in. I long to see my children live in the freedom that Christ died to give them. Thank you, Lord, for godly parents who will not succumb to the drum of the world's beat.

We need to be continuously assessing our decision making for our families to see if it aligns with scripture. To the world, living holy is a dragnet, but to Christians, it should be our target.

A frame that will aim for distinction does not make decisions haphazardly. I encourage you to pray over your decisions for your family by asking yourself, "Will this preferred deny God's Word?"

Where are the women and men who will remain disciplined even if thrown in a (spiritual) lion's den? Let's connect back again to Daniel, shall we? He had a disciplined prayer life. He was told it could not be that way, but he continued to pray three times a day. How would heaven describe your prayer life? Distinct or extinct? Ouch!

Daniel's flame was unstoppable. Although he was pressured not to pray, he was determined not to sway or delay from a set apart prayer life. If we are not careful, we will allow the pressure of hectic schedules to remove our eyes off the importance of prayer.

So do a self-reflection for a minute. How do you represent a flame of distinction in your place of employment? The Father's intent is for you to cement. We have to learn how to stand firmly and boldly for our beliefs that are based on the Word. We can't allow dents in our convictions. If you don't want a dent, make sure your thoughts aren't for rent. Choose distinctive thoughts that can't be bought with silver.

In addition, a flame of distinction is an archer with diligent hands. In Proverbs 21:5, the wisest man in the Bible tells us, "The plans of the diligent lead to profit." God took David from the sheep pens to be the shepherd of his people because he was a flame with "integrity of heart" and "skillful hands" (Ps 78:72).

In Proverbs 6:6, Solomon tells us that we should consider the ant's ways. Personally, I think ants have a spirit of distinction and diligence. They don't just stick to lifting things that are their size. They can actually lift things that are twenty times their size. Pretty impressive, huh? What purpose has God entrusted your hands with that is much bigger than yourself?

If you keep a diligent spirit, you can count on God to show up with supernatural strength to help you push upward. After all, doesn't God tell us that we can bench-press temptations?

While you are nodding yes, flip to 1 Corinthians 10:13. "But when you are tempted, he will also provide a way out so that you can stand up under it." Isn't that what the ant is doing? The small little ant is bench-pressing things stronger than it is.

I think it is interesting to note that ants also fight to their death. I think it is fair to say that, every time I fight a fleshly desire and win, death to carnality takes place, and a spirit of distinction rises to the top. Then I am able to keep pressing "toward the goal to win the prize for which God has called me heavenward in Christ Jesus" (Phil 3:14). Like soldier ants, God has called us to protect and defend our aim while attacking the enemy colonies that want to dominate God's territory.

While we are on the trail of ant trivia, let's shine a little light on the carpenter ant? How in the world did this ant get this name? A carpenter ant builds a nest in pieces of wood. My friend, you and I can have a fiery aim because the Son of the Carpenter gave His life on a piece of wood. He made and then died on a piece of wood so we could have eternal life with Him.

If your aim is excellence and distinction, you will become a spiritual carpenter ant. Workers in this family get the important job of collecting food to feed the next generation. Shouldn't that be the aim of every worker in the kingdom? Like the altar of incense, I pray we will have such a distinction that our flames "will burn regularly before the LORD for the generations to come" (Exod 30:8).

Now, we just can't close this ant discussion without addressing those fire ants. What do you think? Are they distinct? Every time I step into a bed of them, I get the blisters to prove it. They do not waste any time letting you know that you're in their territory. Shouldn't we be like that? That old twister (Satan) needs to feel the blister every time he steps inside God's territory. He should feel the fiery bed whenever he steps inside your fiery red, which is an area of righteousness, excellence, and distinction.[4]

I have concluded that a spirit of distinction will respond quickly. God loves an immediate response. How many times does God have to nudge you to give a larger amount of offering than what you had anticipated? Is your ear so in tuned with God's voice that you respond to the needs around you immediately? God is looking for some fire ants that are aggressive when it comes to a spirit of distinction.

I hope you will take the time to really think about your family's aim. I pray that your aim will be so targeted to truth that your children will never believe the big bang, wild gang, or lie from the fang of the serpent. If you want to live with God's best, you must be committed to the growth of righteousness, excellence, and distinction. What are the flickering lights on your tree that God wants to revolutionize?

God has given each one of us gifts and abilities to use to build the kingdom. He has also given up specific directions in how to be successful with daily tasks. Colossians 3:23 explains, "Whatever you do, work at it

---

[4] "Ants-Facts about Ants-Types of Ants," http://www.petsworldforkids.org/ ants.html

with all your heart, as working for the Lord, not for men, since you know that you will receive an inheritance from the Lord as a reward." When you bend down to pick up trash off the floor at church, cook supper for the sick, or stand against popular opinion that contradicts God's Word, you can do it with zeal because you're working for the Lord.

We need to remind ourselves that we will give an account of our frame and its aim of **r**ighteousness, **e**xcellence, and **d**istinction. If you ever forget that, just turn to Romans 14:12, 2 Corinthians 5:10, 1 Peter 4:5, 2 Timothy 4:1, Hebrews 4:13, and Revelation 22:12.

What exactly makes us lose sight of the "red" aim and ultimately stumble in darkness? I think it happens when we start to believe the absurd and take our eyes off God's Word. Psalm 19:8 says, "The commands of the LORD are radiant, giving light to the eyes." When His Word is my aim, I will always have a "lamp to my feet and a light for my path" (Ps 119:105).

Before we close this chapter, I want us to look at some people who were drawn to aim.

1. **Nehemiah 1-7: Nehemiah.** This man was deeply grieved about the condition of the city, Jerusalem. Nehemiah fasted and prayed for God's direction. He had a humble dependence on God that gave him an aim to rebuild the city's walls. Though faced with opposition, Nehemiah focused his head on the red and completed the task God had given him. Like Nehemiah, you may have a mission that looks impossible, but your set aim will help you to flame on to complete the good work God has started in you.

2. **2 Kings 2: Elisha.** I love the aim of his flame. He wanted a double portion. That's how I've learned to pray, "Lord, give me double for my trouble!" Elisha was a man of force and might, and he wanted to be an incandescent light. His aim can be found in 2 Kings 2:9 when he said to Elijah, "Let me inherit a double portion of your spirit." When you ask God to give you that kind of a flame, you can expect Him to use you incredibly.

3. **1 Samuel 25:1-42: Abigail.** Beauty and brains were extremely strong flames with Abigail. In this chapter, we find here a woman

who had an aim to be a life speaker. David wasn't having a very good day, but Ms. Flame was about to move his way. And she was going to speak life over his difficult situation. Although David was very close to reaching his dreams, he was about to mess up with thoughts to kill Naboth. Abigail was a beautiful and smart woman who feared the Lord. She was a flame who chose to aim at speaking life and dreams back inside David. 1 Samuel 25:24 tells us that Abigail "fell at his feet" and said, "My Lord, let the blame be on me alone." I can just picture her thinking, "I'll be the flame that takes the blame if that's what it takes to remind David of his name, the anointed one." That is the exact attitude we should have toward others. This reminds me of what Paul said in 1 Corinthians 9:22, "I have become all things to all men so that by all possible means I might save some." Take the time to listen to other's dreams and help them push toward the goal line.

As the body of Christ, we should be protective of our own football dreams and hold them tightly to our chest as we head straight for touchdown. Run past the yanking, push past the tripping, and aim your flame. Respond to all the small and big decisions with a holy aim. Take your focus off popular opinion and on to God's dominion. Christ bled for your red!

When your flame has an aim:

1. God gets your best.
2. God gets your zest.
3. God gets your faith in every test.
4. God's bosom is your rest.
5. God is your life vest.
6. God's Word is your nest.
7. God's desires are your quest.
8. In God's people, you will invest.
9. God's thoughts will fill your treasure chest.
10. God's glory will manifest.
11. Sin will stir you like a hornet's nest.

BIBLE STUDY IDEAS

CONNECT[5]

Play the Flame Game. Divide into four groups. Each group is given a brown paper bag. As a group, you must aim to find objects in that room that begin with the letters of these words: We Must Take Aim. You can only use things you can find in the room you are presently in. For example, you could ball up a piece of paper and list it under "t" for trash. Place all objects inside a designated bag, and record the object's name below. The group who gets back to the start line first with the most objects is the winner. Get creative. Work fast. Have fun with your group!

W _____

E _____

M _____

U _____

S _____

T _____

T _____

A _____

K _____

E _____

A _____

I _____

M _____

DIRECT

Share with your group a highlighted thought that ministered to you.

REFLECT

- What are some of your personal convictions or maybe even some new convictions that God has recently placed on your

---

[5]   Idea from the free game archive, www.TheSource 4YM.com

heart that will help you to take aim and flame? What scriptures can you find to support them?

- Satan tries hard to hinder your aim to flame by using regret from the past. What does Paul encourage us to do in in Philippians 3:13?
- What are some things you are asking God to do in your life to help you aim with a fiery flame?
- Read Romans 12:2. How can you renew your mind daily to focus on your aim?
- What are your physical aims? What are your financial aims? What are your family aims?
- Research the following scriptures: 1 Corinthians 9:27, Colossians 3:5, Hebrews 12:1, James 1:21, and 1 Peter 2:11. What are some of the action verbs that we have to do to stay focused on our aim to flame?

COLLECT

Research the following scriptures: Philippians 4:8, 1 Thessalonians 4:7, and 1 Thessalonians 5:6. Take the time to read these with your group. Share your insight. How will these scriptures help you focus on being a frame with an aim?

AFFECT

Take the time to get with your accountability partner. Share a spiritual aim that you want your partner to agree with you in prayer about.

Satan, the Hinderer, may build a barrier about us, but he can never roof us in, so that we cannot look up.

J. Hudson Taylor

CHAPTER 5

Beware of the Enemy's Game

Welcome to Alligator 101. I hope this course will be a special resource for you to gain information on how to guard your flame from the alligator's game. But before proceeding with our alligator quest, we must stop and take an alligator test. Let's see what you know about these crafty creatures.

TRUE OR FALSE

- Alligators are able to survive in saltwater for extended periods of time. ✓ True ✓ False
- The most basic instinct of an alligator is to swim. ✓ True ✓ False
- An alligator swallows its food under the water. ✓ True ✓ False

If you selected false to these questions, you are correct. What does all of that have to do with being a flame? Hang tight. We'll get there. I promise I have a connection within this selection.

THE GAME AFTER YOUR FLAME

Through the pages to come, I hope you will begin to recognize the game that is after your flame. God wants to bless you with a life that will thrill and fulfill you. However, you must be wise and realize the disguise of the enemy. Like an alligator, Satan tries to sneak up on his prey. We must be aware of the game that targets our aim. Let's look at some alligator facts.[6]

First, Satan is after your salt. Alligators are not fond of salt. Not a bit. They lack the salt-extracting glands of crocodiles. Therefore, they are unable to survive in the saltwater for an extended period of time. Like the gator, Satan's eye continues to spy your salty splash to tell others about Christ. The gator's game is to smash and leave you with a gash. Now, halt from that thought on salt and say this with me, "Satan likes fault; he does not like salt."

Satan can't tolerate it when you and I operate in the witnessing mode. In Matthew 5:13, Jesus said, "You are the salt of the earth. But if the salt loses its saltiness, how can it be made salty again? It is no longer good for anything, except to be thrown out and trampled by men." Satan's game for every flame is to remove your flavor to the world, your seasoning packet. He wants to trip you so you will be a tasteless residue that forgets to renew your mind in Christ.

Satan's aim is to make the flame break the salt covenant of loyalty. If you remember the beautiful painting of *The Last Supper*, you have to zoom in on the saltshaker. It reveals a spilling of disloyalty to the Master by Judas. One of Jesus's very own disciples stood at the edge of the bank and down, down, down he sank. The alligator's snout took him out. Judas fell for the gator's game and lost his purpose to aim and flame for Christ.

Satan knows the power of salt. If you feel like your flame has died, begin praying for a new deep-fried desire to "taste and see that the LORD is good" (Ps 34:8). When all feels dead and you're fighting the dread, cry out from your soul for a new bowl of salt. It brings wholesomeness to your life. That's exactly what Elijah did.

Turn with me to 2 Kings 2:19. In this story, we find "the water is bad and the land is unproductive." Notice Elijah's response in 2 Kings 2:20, "'Bring me a new bowl,' he said, 'and put salt in it.'" What was the outcome? "And the water has remained wholesome to this day, according to the word Elisha had spoken" (2 Kgs 2:22). Satan's groove is to remove your salt from being a blessing to those around you. Don't fall for the gator's game.

---

6   "Ask Old Pete (Croc Expert)—Alligator and Fur Council," www.alligatorfur.com/edu/pete.htm

Second, Satan is after your thoughts. He would like nothing better than to eat you up with a cup of pride. Satan will continue to eat to put distance between your feet and God's seat of priority in your life. The enemy knows how God feels about pride. "Though the LORD is on high, he looks upon the lowly, but the proud he knows from afar" (Ps 138:6). Satan is just like the fox in *The Gingerbread Man*. He wants you to come up higher so he can gobble you down lower.

Friend, God has a clear word for His bride about pride. "God opposes the proud but gives grace to the humble" (James 4:6). Satan is a mastermind at setting traps of a haughty spirit in your life. 1 Peter 5:8 tells us that Satan is looking for someone to devour. His game includes a light, camera, and action ride that causes an enormous amount of pride.

Third, Satan is after your ought. Alligators know the power of waiting. They camouflage themselves, sit quietly, and wait for sounds and movement. The enemy operates just like that. He waits for you to verbalize your thoughts so he can slap and trap with a big ol' gap. When you hold ought against someone, there is distance and resistance to God's target for your life. Satan camouflages ought so you fail to see his spirit working behind that offense. Don't take the bait of hate. Don't fall into the claws and jaws of the alligator. Have you ever found yourself screaming, "It's just not fair that I have to forgive them"? As we mature in Christ, we learn to relinquish the bitterness grenade for a marvelous upgrade of blessings. When we lay down our life (Matt 16:24), we lay down all strife. Satan can't give a "cursey" (curse) when you're giving "mercy" to those who have hurt you.

How interesting that alligators have a transparent third eyelid that helps with its view when submerged underwater. It works very much like swimming goggles. The gator can't see too well with this third eye, but it can recognize light and darkness. Likewise, the enemy knows there is a strong connection with the light and spiritual eyesight. Matthew 6:22-23 says, "The eye is the lamp of the body. If your eyes are good, your whole body will be full of light. But if your eyes are bad, your whole body will be full of darkness." Our eye must rely on God. If our eyes are focused on being proud or following the crowd, we can expect a cloud to settle down over our effectiveness. If you don't have spiritual vision, you'll end up with a collision with the gator. Dig in your pockets deep, because collision with bitterness is never cheap.

Satan wants your flaw resting on his jaw, which brings me to another point. Did you know the alligator's tongue is attached to its bottom jaw? The upper jaw must stay in place. Therefore, the alligator has to lift up his head in order to devour his prey. Yippee! Good news for you and me! Before Satan can try to eat at my family tree, he must get specific permission from Thee.

If you have fallen in his trap and you're feeling the snap, cry out, "Help me, Jesus!" And when you do, the alligator hears the same words the big fish did in the book of Jonah, "Spit him out!"

Hebrews 2:18 says, "Because he himself suffered when he was tempted, he is able to help those who are being tempted." Jesus runs to the cries of His people who call out to Him. No matter where you are, His grace will run to embrace you. No matter the quirk, God's amazing grace is always at work.

Jesus is our example of how to handle the gator. Turn with me to Matthew 4. Here, we see the game plan to attack God's precious flame, Jesus. Let's investigate the strategies Satan used then and is still using today in our lives.

The Aim Targeted at Your Flame

Drought

Jesus had been fasting forty days and forty nights when the tempter started up his game. Satan knows the power of attacking us when we are tired and lonely. Just as the body needs food, our soul needs fuel. Satan doesn't want us attending a church where the Holy Spirit is in charge. He wants us in dry places so we fail to receive the revelation of God. His game for your flame is to always keep you dry from God Most High. Satan doesn't want you to have intimate time in prayer and applying what you have heard from His Word. Jesus was able to resist the enemy's plan by applying the Word through the drought season.

Route

Satan is always trying to get you away from your mission route. In this temptation scene, we see how Satan was after the mission of Christ. Satan would have liked nothing better than for Jesus to have declared his kingship before His time. How did Jesus respond to the game? He simply obeyed the Word of God. It's one thing to know the Word but another to walk it out. We must be aware of the "gator holes" that Satan has dug out for our lives.

I also find it interesting that alligators use their mouth, tail, claws, and legs to uproot vegetation and dig out gator holes. Satan never wants you to plant. If you plant, you will not gallivant. He loves it when you go "to and fro," like Satan did in the book of Job. One church to another. One marriage to another. More houses. More blouses. More spouses. Satan knows that those who are "planted in the house of the Lord" get to "flourish in the courts of God" (Ps 92:13).

The gator hole always offers an imitation of the real deal. It's filled with deceit aimed straight for your feet. Satan fights with a mask of disguise and a claw filled with lies to capture your light.

2 Corinthians 11:14 warns us that "Satan himself masquerades as an angel of light." Satan wants your feet stuck in the gator holes because he knows "how beautiful on the mountains are the feet of those who bring good news, who proclaim peace, who bring good tidings, who proclaim salvation" (Isa 52:7).

Don't ever stop believing that God truly cares about your physical and spiritual gator holes. I nursed a grudge and woke up to find myself in a gator hole. I learned you can't win a soul when you are stuck in a gator hole. When you fall in the alligator's clutch, you lose your touch to affect others with your flame. His bite will hide your light. Satan will snap and zap all your energy when you hold ought against anyone.

Friend, gator holes will always cater to you. The gator is very crafty at sending a barrage of enticements that are always filled with excitement (temporarily). Gator holes will suck you down with celebration sounds. However, Satan's intent is to destroy you. Proverbs 14:12 says, "There is a way that seems right to a man, but in the end it leads to death."

We must look past Satan's game and see that gator holes are after our aim. Gator holes are after your freedom. Ephesians 5:15 says, "Be careful, then, how you live—not as unwise but as wise, making the most of every opportunity, because the days are evil." Satan wants you on the route of careless living, low self-esteem, deformed desires, discontentment, fear, adultery, pornography, depression, addictions, and secretive entertainment. If God's Word says it's wrong, run as fast as you can from that gator hole. As a flame, you should "prepare your minds for action" in how you will deal with the gator hole aimed at your soul (1 Pet 1:13).

HOLDOUT

Satan wants your worship. He crawls toward the devout with a spirit to hold out. Satan is after supreme control to keep your name off heaven's roll. If he can, Satan will enslave all the way to the grave. Don't hold back on God. May the Holy Spirit help us to have a God-directed enthusiasm to put the pedal to the metal and go after the hot spot with all we have.

I firmly believe that Jesus is drawing us into loving Him more passionately. The more you love Him, the more you shove sin. Push the nasty bait back in that nasty plate. In order to be a light, ask for a change of appetite. Every day, we should fold our menus and say, "I'll have whatever the Father is having today."

God wants us to know the alligator's game. He even tells us in Matthew 6:9-13 to pray, "And lead us not into temptation, but deliver us from the evil one." James 1:13-14 reminds us that "when tempted, no one should say, 'God is tempting me.'" Our own attraction to the gator hole tempts us.

My prayer is that you will become more alert to gator holes. 2 Timothy 2:22 says, "Flee the evil desires of youth, and pursue righteousness, faith, love and peace." I pray you will begin to spot the gator holes in your life. Learn to use self-control and refuse that gator hole. You will not become Satan's dessert if you stay alert. 1Thessalonians 5:6 says, "But let us be alert and self-controlled." If you don't stay actively alert, you're going down in the dirt.

Proverbs 4:23 says, "Above all else, guard your heart, for it is the wellspring of life." People in parts of Florida understand the importance of a guard. Many have to put up fences to keep the alligators out of their pools. I have to keep pounding this point. If you will stay on guard, you can keep the gator out of your yard. "Be on your guard; stand firm in the faith; be men of courage; be strong" (1 Cor 16:13). If we become comfortable or tolerable of any sin in our lives, Satan has a foothold. Hook in mouth. An entry point that disappoints our Savior.

Your frame will never flame to its potential until you deal with free will. Jesus has issued dos and don'ts in His Word. We choose to obey or not. We have the choice to walk with Him or walk away from Him.

Don't ever forget that the enemy is an experienced marcher and archer. He is very cunning when targeting your aim. However, I believe God desires to train us to protect our flame. Psalm 18:34 says, "He trains my hands for battle." God does not promise to eliminate challenges and combativeness, but He does promise to teach us how to fight with His might. In order to overcome the temptation of gator holes, we should consider the following.

SEEK A MIND

We need to be seeking a mind that the Holy Spirit controls. The gator is out to terrorize and traumatize. God's Spirit will tenderize and energize us to reflect the image of God. We must "have the mind of Christ" in order to walk out His mission on earth victoriously (1 Cor 2:16). A mind controlled by the Spirit will learn something new from an eternal view. If we neglect to seek His mind, our purpose will never be defined and headlined. When God gets the rein to your mind, He can refine you as pure as gold. Get plugged into ministry and hold yourself accountable for your actions. Your flame will swell when you force your mind to dwell on God's desires. Satan will get your glow when you focus on things below. Therefore, "set your minds on things above, not on earthly things" (Col 3:2).

REMOVE THE BLIND

Our culture is invading our home with ungodly things. We glamorize things like money, power, witchcraft, violence, and so forth. 2 Corinthians 4:4 says, "The god of this age has blinded the minds of unbelievers, so that they cannot see the light of the gospel of the glory of Christ, who is the image of God." Satan wants you and I confined to be blind. But God longs to give spiritual discernment. Jesus will heal any blind eye and deadened heart if they will turn to Him (John 12:40). God longs to open our spiritual eyes to see the fire of His protection, just like He did for Elisha's servant (2 Kgs 6:17). We need to have a consistent message to the enemy, "Get thee behind; you're not getting in my mind!"

FOSTER DESIRES THAT ARE ALIGNED

We are called to be a set apart for Christ. Our desires need to align with the Father's heart. Romans 12:1 says you are "to offer your bodies as living sacrifices, holy and pleasing to God." We should not want to live in such a way that our sacrifices become unholy. Turn to Leviticus 10 to learn this from two men. Nadab and Abihu, sons of Aaron, died because they offered "unauthorized fire before the LORD" (Lev 10:1). Our lives must foster desires that align with God's truth.

FEAR OF THE LORD HEADLINED

I'm not talking about being afraid of Jesus. I'm talking about a godly fear. The Bible is filled with scriptures to remind us of the connections between fear of the Lord and blessings. Psalm 111:10 says, "The fear of the LORD is the beginning of wisdom; all who follow his precepts have good understanding." Would you agree that fear and feelings are always in stiff competition? The winner of the two determines your acceleration into all God has planned for you. Let's look at characters in the Bible for some examples here. Let's discuss the Mr. Js and Mr. As.

In Genesis 39, Joseph experienced a temptation that is running rampant today, adultery. Potiphar's wife was filled with deceit and threw herself at Joseph's feet. How did Mr. J respond to this temptation? Joseph says in Genesis 39:9, "How then could I do such a wicked thing and sin against God?" It's pretty clear that godly fear won that round, hands down.

What about Job? Job 1:1 was clear that "he feared God and shunned evil." Job gives us quite an insight about how to handle temptation. Stand clear and veer by choosing to fear God.

Now let's go the opposite direction as we head for Genesis with Adam. A lack of godly fear will always cause you to take a bite even though it's not right. Satan will always offer an appeal to what seems to be a tasty meal. When we give in to the feel, we break the seal of communion with Christ. Adam ate because the feeling was great toward the gator's bait. And fear came too late. If we make decisions based upon feelings, we will always gravitate toward sin. We would be much better off if we would fear more and feel less.

Now, let's check out Ahab. 1 Kings 16:30 tells us that Ahab "did more evil in the eyes of the Lord than any of those before him." Ahab lacked the fear of the Lord. Without fear, you don't have the gear to fight warfare of the soul. If your only armor is feeling, be prepared. You will lose your breath and experience death from the gator.

Before we close this chapter, I want us to look at some more people who fell for the game and lost their flame.

1. **Judges 13-16: Samson.** Samson had great potential. However, he fell for the game of self-confidence, self-indulgence, and self-reliance. The bottom line is that we will never be a match to the enemy when we fight with our own strength. That is why

we need to be listening to the sweet Holy Spirit. If deception and interception is the gator's strategy, perception needs to be ours.

2. **1 Kings 11: Solomon.** King David's son started out with a flame of wisdom. However, his flame soon dwindled down from the gator's game of self-sufficiency, self-satisfaction, and self-destruction. Ecclesiastes allows us to the peer into the mind of a dimly burning wick that came to realize how meaningless life will become when you fall for the gator's game.

As a flame, we must know how to react to the gator's game of sin. We must crash it, bash it, and smash it. Take it down. Hold sin's shoulder to the floor and cry aloud, "Gator, no more! No more will you trap me there." With a tight grip, count one, two, three. "That will teach you to mess with me," you will say.

We must have stamping feet with fiery heat toward any encroachment of sin. Satan will persist where a stronghold exists. His rule is to destroy, but his tool is to employ us to the company of sin. If the alligator can divide, it will affect how you reside close to the Father's heart. May your flame be quick to recognize the gator's trick.

When you are facing a temptation, think about the following:

- If I do this, will it affect my sleep?
- If I do this, will it affect my leap?
- If I do this, will sin begin to creep?
- If I do this, will it make the Father weep?

BIBLE STUDY IDEAS

CONNECT[7]
Divide up in groups of three: Team A, Team B, and Team C. Pass out three dry erase boards and markers to record answers. Team A sends a member of their group to the front. He must be ready to trick the other groups. He must share three sentences about himself. Two must be true.

---

[7] Satan uses gator holes to trap us to believe a lie. Gator holes are false traps. Let's play the Gator Hole Game! (Idea from the free game archive, www. thesource4ym.com/GAMES).

One statement must be a gator hole, or a false statement. The other two groups listen and record the statement they believe is inaccurate on the dry erase board labeled "Gator Hole." The group that locates the gator hole statement gets a point and sends a member of their group to the front. If neither group finds the gator hole, Team A gets the point. The team with the most points when time is called is the winner. Look out for those gator holes!

DIRECT
Share with your group a highlighted thought that ministers to you.

REFLECT
- What are some examples of gator holes?
- What are some feelings that we might experience that would cause us to fall into a gator hole? What are some things we should do the very moment a gator hole thought enters our mind? Satan's game often involves a clever imitation of the real deal. What characters in the Bible fell for a clever imitation? What was the outcome?
- What other characteristics or habits of an alligator is similar to the work of Satan?
- Name some preventative maintenance ideas that will help keep us away from gator holes.
- Read Mark 11:25-26. What gator hole is Jesus warning us about? If comfortable, share about your experience with this gator hole and how God has helped you to overcome.

COLLECT
Research the following scriptures: Matthew 26:41, 1 Corinthians 10:12-13, Hebrews 4:15 and 12:1, and 1 Peter 5:8. Take the time to read these with your group. Share your insight. How will these help you focus on being a frame who is aware of Satan's game?

AFFECT
Take the time to get with an accountability partner. Pray specifically for a gator hole in your life such as fear, self-sufficiency, and so forth. Pray that your partner will be able to see any gator holes in the future.

Words, so innocent and powerless . . . when standing in a dictionary, how potent for good or evil they become in the hands of one who knows how to combine them.

Nathaniel Hawthorne

CHAPTER 6

Aim and Claim

When was the last time you had a yearly checkup or any type of doctor's visit? I hear you. It's not my favorite thing to do either. But at least today's visit will be free, so come along with me and jump on the doctor's table. Imagine with me, the Great Physician listening to your concerns about your frustrated symptoms. You can go ahead and point to your heart space, but His eyes will focus on the face. It never fails. Whether old or young, you're going to hear the words, "Stick out your tongue."

Our Great Physician knows that, to have a heart that is brand new, He must address the tongue issue. I don't know about you, but I get so aggravated when I burn my tongue from eating hot food. I pay for it the rest of the day. However, I've come to realize the reason I burned my tongue was because I lacked patience. If I had just waited for that baked potato to cool some more, I wouldn't have a tongue so sore. Likewise, if we could learn to wait for feelings to cool before speaking, we wouldn't have so many people with burnt lives from hot-tempered words.

Like Abraham, God can use us to spread blessings to the "west and to the east, to the north and to the south," but, oh my goodness, it must start with our mouth (Gen 28:14). If we desire to be a body of both physical and spiritual health, we must daily claim God's promises over our lives. If we want to be a catalyst in which God uses to help others to freedom, we must learn to illuminate the positive and eliminate the negative.

Our tongue will always struggle with craving power. Pride and gossip are all wrapped up in this power struggle. Why do you think so much gossip is running rampant? People feel powerful when they think they know something about another person. Why do so many people try to belittle you as they brag about themselves? If you guess the right answer, I'll give you a star. It starts with a "p" and ends with an "r." What makes so many people have such a rebellious tongue? Give up? It's called the tower of "power." People feel a great sense of power when they put others down.

God has written many prescriptions in His Word for addressing the tongue issue. If we want to be instrumental, we must keep our tongue controlled, very bold, like apples of gold, and from being cold. Let's look at these four a little bit more.

PREPARE THE TONGUE TO AIM

KEEP OUR TONGUE CONTROLLED
Every year, I join many of you in starting my year off with a twenty-one-day fast. I have learned so much from Pastor Jentezen Franklin about the power of prayer and fasting. One year, God showed me that, along with food, I was to fast an attitude called criticism. Maybe you've mastered this area, but I have lots of room for improvement. For the entire month of January, I was challenged to fast words of criticism along with my regular fast. I really began to notice how often my flesh was tempted to speak a negative thought. Now, there is a stronger conviction toward speaking criticism that has birthed inside of me from fasting. When my tongue is tempted to speak too quickly, I must remember that "a man of understanding holds his tongue" (Prov 11:12). I believe the Spirit is drawing us to greater maturity as we learn, "He who guards his lips guards his life, but he who speaks rashly will come to ruin" (Prov 13:3). I really encourage you to sign up for the criticism fast. It's powerful! We must claim self-control over the words we speak.

KEEP OUR TONGUE BOLD
An aim with a fiery flame must never be ashamed to share Christ with others. Our flame will stand tall if we follow the steps of Paul. This man shared his faith with others (Acts 28:31). He declared his faith to others (Acts 16:22-25). He prepared His faith for others through a bold ministry. May we daily pray, "Enable your servants to speak your word with great boldness" (Acts 4:29). The Holy Spirit wants to help us speak with valor as He did in Acts. "And they were all filled with the Holy

Spirit and spoke the word of God boldly" (Acts 4:31). We must claim boldness over the words we speak.

Keep Our Tongue like Apples of Gold

Your life has the greatest potential to produce overflowing baskets of fruit if you will postulate and think abundance. Your words are precious seeds to every situation. Proverbs 25:11 says, "A word aptly spoken is like apples of gold in settings of silver." New revelation hits me every time I read Proverbs 18:21, which says, "The tongue has the power of life and death, and those who love it will eat its fruit." I want to be drawn to aim at choosing thoughts that will be a blessing to others. As a Christian, God has pulled you out of the muck, so don't go back to living stuck.

We can't afford to get stuck in a habit of speaking unconstructively. We must choose to think favor minded. Don't think frail. Jesus took your nail to keep you from hell. Even when you fail, God will graciously put you back on the holy trail because you are the head not the tail (Deut 28:13). Yeah! That's right.

Stop reversing and start dispersing the seed of God's Word. "The seed is the Word of God" (Luke 8:11). We absolutely must stop speaking pessimistically about ourselves and others. Our prayers should be genuine excitement for what God is doing now and what he is going to do in our future.

According to quotesbuddy.com, Robert H. Schuller once said, "Any fool can count the seeds in an apple. Only God can count all the apples in one seed." We need to respond to the drawing of the Spirit to become a seed packet that makes a lot of racket about the goodness of the Lord. According to wisdomcommons.org, an unknown author once said, "A candle loses nothing of its light by lighting another candle." Therefore, we should always be ready to use our flame to light another's candle with encouraging words. We must claim positive thoughts over our lives and the lives of others.

Keep Our Tongue from Being Cold

King David shared powerful wisdom in Psalm 39:1, "I will watch my ways and keep my tongue from sin; I will put a muzzle on my mouth." We have fallen for Satan's bait if we choose to enter the gossip gate. Proverbs 16:28 says, "A perverse man stirs up dissension and a gossip separates close friends." We can't be an army that will stoop to hurt his own group. Proverbs 11:9 says, "With his mouth the godless destroys his neighbor."

When you see someone struggling in some area of ministry, don't criticize. Realize that God may be guiding you to mentor them. Graciously pull up a seat beside him and encourage him with a spirit of gentleness. If you want your ministry to grow, make sure you have encouraging words that flow. James 1:26 reminds us, "If anyone considers himself religious and yet does not keep a tight rein on his tongue, he deceives himself and his religion is worthless."

God desires to give us influence, but our words must align with His. The more you know Him, the more you will believe and speak His heart. When our words claim God's truth, it's sweet to the soul and nourishing to the heart. Our light involves claiming God's Word. Luke 8:16 says, "No one lights a lamp and hides it in a jar or puts it under a bed. Instead, he puts it on a stand, so that those who come in can see the light." When we are not aligning our speech with God's infallible Word, we are hiding light.

DECLARE THE TONGUE TO AIM

Have you noticed how we often allow our tongue to flop when we meet a roadblock because of a rock? In Numbers 20, God gave Moses a technique when it comes to rocky places. The technique was to speak. Then a miracle would leak. But Moses chose to hit rather than submit. God is looking for a flame who will claim His Word over every obstacle he faces and allow His work to shine through him. Job 22:28 says, "What you decide on will be done, and light will shine on your ways."

At every rock situation, our frame needs to speak miracles by using positive words. If you claim negative with your tongue, like Moses, you've just swung.

When I am negative, my focus is on me. When I am positive, my focus is on Thee. Grab your binoculars to find the focus of Moses's question to the Israelites in Numbers 20:10, "Must we bring you water out of this rock?" Can you imagine God saying, "Pardon me, but what is this we?" God is the only one who can bring the overflow. What spring-filled gush do we crush because we rush on the scene with disobedience, negativity, or a prideful tongue?

The bottom line is that your frame must choose to use speech that will reach out and grab your destiny. When the world speaks nope, you speak hope. When the world speaks strife, you speak life. We must claim God's truth in our hearts "for out of the overflow of the heart the mouth speaks" (Matt 12:34).

We can't afford to get into a routine of being unclean with our tongue. Jesus said in Matthew 15:11, "What goes into a man's mouth does not make him unclean, but what comes out of his mouth, that is what makes him unclean." We need to be moving forward by fixing our eyes on what God says about our lives. Isaiah 59:21 has a specific word for us about the mouth. "My Spirit, who is on you, and my words that I have put in your mouth will not depart from your mouth, or from the mouths of your children, or from the mouths of their descendants from this time on and forever."

May you be filled with zeal knowing God will fulfill the prayers of those who pray for His spirit to be poured out in these last days. In Numbers 11:29, we see that Moses prayed for God's spirit to be poured out. Many generations later in the book of Acts, we see that exact prayer fulfilled. I pray you will be drawn to a desire for God's spirit to be poured out upon your flame so you can move forward with His aim.

There's no doubt about it. If you complain, you'll remain. But when you bless, here comes success. We need to be professing things over our lives that are true, noble, right, pure, lovely, admirable, excellent, and praiseworthy (Phil 4:8). We need to be sunflowers that are bending to God's sending with words of encouragement. Jesus is your reason to always want to season every conversation with salt (Col 4:6).

Who will be in heaven because your fruit revealed His peace, His joy, and His goodness? Let's go deeper. Who will be in heaven because your fruit was squeezed or pressed like an olive yet your lip chose to drip with anointed words? Your commitment to Christ is most evident to others when you can still speak about the goodness of the Lord in the face of affliction. My friend, you are anointed and appointed, and the enemy wants you disjointed. Our negative words will disjoint us from miracles.

A frame that claims words of life will become so sensitive to the voice of the Lord. If the words that you're about to speak aren't going to benefit its audience, don't say it. Simply put, if God didn't stamp it, you better clamp it. Don't deliver anything out of your mouth that doesn't have God's stamped approval on it.

In the midst of your doubt or drought, learn to shout under the spout and hold out. In the drab, learn to grab the horns of the altar and speak life over your situation. Jesus tells us in John 11:25, "I am the resurrection and the life." Speak resurrection over your circumstance. Speak resurrection over your sickness. Speak resurrection over your marriage or finances. When you grab God's promises with your tongue, you stab and jab the enemy in the lung. We must allow God to shape our flame on His Word and shape His Word in our flame. Amen!

FRESH AIR FOR THOSE WHO CLAIM

CLAIM INCREASE

I believe God is drawing us to increase our love for one another so that speaking positive will become a natural habit. 1 Thessalonians 3:12 says, "May the Lord make your love increase and overflow for each other." Fire does not stay in one place, does it? It moves and proves how strong it really is. Love is a fire that God approves and moves into taller flames. As we allow God's love to become our centerpiece, our love for others will rapidly increase and have great impact on our words.

CLAIM PEACE

"You will keep in perfect peace him whose mind is steadfast because he trusts in you" (Isa 26:3). When the hurricanes of life strike your family, what foundation will you have that will stand the wind? Proverbs 24:3 says, "By wisdom a house is built, and through understanding it is established; through knowledge its rooms are filled with rare and beautiful treasures." The foundation of our soul affects the whole. I believe that my family's vitality is affected by whether or not my husband and I choose to build our house on a secure foundation.

Isaiah 33:6 says that Jesus "will be the sure foundation for your times, a rich store of salvation and wisdom and knowledge." Matthew 7:25 teaches us that our house will not fall when its foundation is on the rock. 1 Corinthians 3:11 reminds us that we can't lay any foundation other than Jesus.

Parents, your child's stability and peace will only come through the Rock, Jesus Christ. As parents, we need to pay close attention to the scripture in Isaiah 54:13, "All your sons will be taught by the LORD, and great will be your children's peace." So many times, we lose our peace and fail to stand because we haven't followed God's command. We often blame God for a lack of peace in our lives when the problem lies within ourselves. "If only you had paid attention to my commands, your peace would have been like a river" (Isa 48:18).

CLAIM RELEASE

God has called us to be a light "to open eyes that are blind, to free captives from prison and to release from the dungeon those who sit in darkness" (Isa 42:7). As we release our hurts and offenses to God, He will help us to encourage others to do the same. I am convinced that what doesn't destroy you will employ you for great things. I have learned that God often allows a sentence of death before a miracle of breath so you will know that He is God. I serve a God that owns the cattle and the moon and can turn a battle into a boon, which means blessing! So claim it. Claim that blessing! Claim that release! Claim that miracle! It doesn't matter that the doctors have said, "We have run out of options for you." Smile through that trial because God is walking every mile with you. Search God's Word and find the promises that match your problems. Post them on your mirror and refrigerator as you fight that agitator of skepticism.

If we want to bring God glory, we have to claim territory. So here's our choice. We can run like a cat up a tree, or we can stand like a lion and trust in Thee. Proverbs 28:1 says, "The wicked man flees though no one pursues, but the righteous are as bold as a lion." Sin will make you a coward and keep you hiding from God's promises.

DARE TO BE A LION

The Bible is packed with many lions that chose to claim their territory instead of running from the enemy. Before we close this chapter, I want us to look at some of those lion spirits who were drawn to be a flame that claimed territory.

1. **Judges 3:31: Shamgar.** This chapter shares a story about a man named Shamgar who refused to run. He claimed his territory and showed he was ready to be used of God any hour of the day.

Shamgar used a simple farm tool, an ox goad, to strike down six hundred Philistines. Shamgar is an example to us that God can choose the "foolish things of the world to shame the wise" (1 Cor 1:27).

2. **2 Samuel 21:1-14: Rizpah.** I just love the passion of the mother in this story. The Bible tells us that Rizpah's sons had been innocently murdered. Their bodies were left on a hill to die. Did she cave in to a hopeless situation? No, she stayed put on a rock, a hard place. What were the results? Rizpah claimed her miracle and got it. Rizpah's sons received a proper burial.

Shamgar and Rizpah were lions. Lions are focused on results. Lions have a loud roar, too. Did you know their roar can be heard up to two miles away? Let's make it personal. How far away can the enemy hear you claiming God's promises over your family?

Who will dare to be a lion? In Micah 5:8, the remnant is referred to as a lion. Even if you have to expose yourself to ridicule, step out on a limb of faith and claim your purpose to flame on. "Be strong and courageous, and do the work. Do not be afraid or discouraged, for the Lord God, my God, is with you. He will not fail you or forsake you" (1 Chr 28:20). In most cases, I've had to speak courage before I felt it. In every circumstance, we can choose a lion's stance. May you forever be drawn to claim your position over the enemy with your positive and courageous words that align with God's promises!

BIBLE STUDY IDEAS

CONNECT[8]

Let's play the Candle Game. Place small birthday candles inside a box. Each participant should be instructed to take out three candles. Every person will share an idea based upon which color of candle he or she pulls out of the box. The group leader should have thought of ideas to match each candle. Here are just some suggestions:

- Pink candle: Share a favorite television program.

---

[8] Idea from www.icebreakers.ws

- White candle: Share a friend quality you admire.
- Yellow candle: Share a favorite food.
- Blue candle: Share a person that you look up to and tell why.

DIRECT
Share with your group a highlighted thought that ministers to you.

REFLECT
- Examine a tube of toothpaste. Explain how words in your mouth are like toothpaste coming out of a tube. Why is it so important that you speak words of life?
- Proverbs 12:14 says, "From the fruit of his lips a man is filled with good things as surely as the work of his hands rewards him." Share some examples in the Bible where positive words changed the outcome of a circumstance. What were some situations where negative words affected a situation?
- How does your choice of words impact your faith?
- Read James 3:3-12. What do these scriptures teach us?
- What are some examples of an untamed tongue?
- If a repeating parrot follows you daily, what words would he repeat from your mouth? Are there some words you want to remove from your tongue? Why?
- Brainstorm creative ways that you can communicate words of love to your husband, children, church members, or colleagues, for example, putting love notes in your child's tennis shoes.
- In Proverbs 6:16, we find things the Lord hates. Discuss these and how many involve the tongue.
- Read Proverbs 12:16. How hard is this for you to do? What could help you to become that prudent man?
- Homework: Write your name on a small slip of paper to be placed in a cup. Each person should draw a name. Write about a character trait that you have noticed and admire about that person since the Bible study started. If there is a visitor to the group, allow his or her friend to do this. Prepare to share at next meeting to encourage one another.

COLLECT

Research the following scriptures: Psalm 19:14, Proverbs 16:23, John 6:63, and Ephesians 4:29. Take the time to read these with your group. Share your insight. How will these help you focus on being a frame with an aim to claim words of life?

AFFECT

Take the time to get with an accountability partner. Pray with your partner about a concern that needs words of life spoken over it.

God is looking for ordinary people empowered by
Him to do extraordinary things!

Unknown

CHAPTER 7

Bring Christ Fame

God is my Creator, and my life is His theater. I want the music to flow all for the Maestro. The theme of my family's life has become the scripture found in Psalm 115:1, "Not to us, O LORD, not to us but to your name be the glory, because of your love and faithfulness." It is obligatory. We must bring Him glory.

By the way, what is glory? According to Merriam-Webster, glory means, "Renown; honor and praise rendered in worship." When we give God glory, we are acknowledging His excellence, His worthiness.

Is your life's passion to become more contagious, courageous, and efficacious for God's glory? Oh, how I want Him to use every scene of my life to display His greatness and awesomeness. I ache for Him to use my weakness and bleakness to demonstrate His resurrecting power.

When you close this chapter, I want your heart to have captured this thought: I do not exist so God can fulfill my "give me" list. I exist to be an enthusiast that brings God glory.

I really believe God is drawing us to produce the "much" fruit His Word speaks of in John 15:8, "This is to my Father's glory, that you bear much fruit, showing yourselves to be my disciples."

I hope while reading this chapter you have a kairos moment, a significant moment where a word is transferred from your head to your heart. When Mary experienced her kairos moment concerning the birth of Jesus, the story was sealed with glory. "Suddenly a great company of the heavenly host appeared with the angel, praising God and saying, 'Glory to God in the highest'" (Luke 2:13-14). I pray your revelation will be sealed with glory as well.

I get so stirred when I read the Word in Psalm 19:1, "The heavens declare the glory of God." You really learn to cling when you realize that everything in your life can be used to bring our Father glory? Even in tragedy? Oh, yeah! Even in tragedy. Even when my heart breaks? Yes. There is not a trauma, travesty, or tribulation that God can't use to bring glory to His name. Psalm 50:15 says, "And call upon me in the day of trouble; I will deliver you, and you will honor me." God is going to do a mighty work in your valley because He promised in Proverbs 16:4, "The Lord works out everything for his own ends."

FLAME ON THROUGH THE TRIAL

I have lived long enough to conclude that life is packed with lots of cracks. But it's then that I consider the pearl. From the oyster shell's perspective, the situation looks defective. If the shell could talk, I wonder if it might say something like, "I think this crack is going to cause a setback."

So what happens when this wonderfully made shell experiences a sand invader because of a crack? What does the oyster do? Its defense mechanism must work hard and smart to release a fluid to coat the irritant. As a result, inside an oyster's dorm, a beautiful pearl begins to form. See the connection? Like an oyster shell, we must see that the cracks in our own lives can make beautiful pearls in the hands of our Creator. Just as layers, light, and time help to form the physical pearl, God can use these same ingredients to bring forth a pearl in our own season of irritants.[9]

If you are going to be a blazing fire, you must trust His "higher" found in Isaiah 55:9. "As the heavens are higher than the earth, so are my ways higher than your ways and my thoughts than your thoughts."

Problems are inevitable. Oh, yes, they are. The question is: Are we going to trust God's view? A bigger picture paints us as the victor. "But thanks be to God, who always leads us in triumphal procession in Christ and through us spreads everywhere the fragrance of the knowledge of him" (2 Cor 2:14). I want to encourage you that God can draw you to a place of holy determination so you will keep on drinking from His healing fountain.

---

9   "How Are Pearls Made?" http://wanttoknowit.com/how-are-pearls-made

The enemy wants you to see problems as a mountain instead of a fountain in which God's unlimited power can flood your life with His promises. Flip to 1 Kings 18:16-45 and take notes from Elijah. Facing Mount Carmel, Elijah chose to see a fountain instead of a mountain. Though tempted to think, "I'm in quite a jam," he chose to trust the God of Abraham. He chose to pray at his mountain, "Let it be known today that you are God in Israel" (1 Kgs 18:36). Elijah saw his mountain as a way to make God famous. I just love the way God showed up with a wham and grand slam of fire. Yeah, God!

Mount Carmel might have got the wham, but Mount Moriah got the ram. Flip back to Genesis 22 and take notes from Abraham. As he headed up Mount Moriah, Abraham knew God was asking him to sacrifice his promised son. Abraham didn't focus on the mountain but rather the fountain of God's supernatural miracle, and he got it.

So let's review this. Mount Carmel got the wham while Mount Moriah got the ram. However, another mountain got the best. Mount Calvary got the Lamb, the great I am. I'm so glad God looked past the mountain of strife so we could receive the Fountain of Life.

FLAME ON THROUGH THE PILE

God is still writing stories of the Bible through your life. Do not toss your story to the curb, but let it become a proverb of wisdom to others. What if the sinful woman would have let her pile of shame affect her flame? She, in fact, gave us a story of what is mandatory. She pushed past opposition to minister to Christ. What stories of your past have you hidden? God wants to remind you in this chapter that He can use anything to bring Him glory. However, you must release that pain to Him. He is calling you to tower through your "this hour," like Jesus did.

In John 12:27, we see the beautiful heart of Christ drawn to bring God all the glory when he said, "Now my heart is troubled, and what shall I say? Father, save me from this hour? No, it was for this very reason I came to this hour. Father, glorify your name."

What an example we have in Christ. We must be drawn to flame on through the pile and walk every mile with our torch aimed high. When you do this, you are an expression of extreme faith. Who will say to you in heaven, "Your sad season was the very reason I gave my life to Christ!

When you walked through that pain not asking Christ to explain but rather choosing to strain, I met the main source of your strength"?

Can Christ trust you to be the spoken reason during your broken season? 1 Corinthians 4:2 says, "Those who have been given a trust must prove faithful." Have you proven to be faithful during times of testing? When your "this hour" comes, you must strap yourself to the surgery table and let God do the work that is needed. God is able to use your season to communicate a love story like no other. A story of restoration.

Like my friend Christle. She is certainly one of the most passionate mothers I know. Christle and Steven invested so much time in teaching their only child, Cailie Grace, all about prayer, giving, fasting, believing, serving others, and learning God's Word. They were doing exactly what God had called them to do. They were aiming that bow and arrow straight toward Christ. However, the day came when it seemed God was pulling back on that arrow in a confusing way. I still remember my exact location when I got the phone call that Cailie Grace, age eight, had been in a car accident. A few hours later, I learned that Cailie Grace was with Jesus.

After Cailie Grace's funeral, my friend Christle was taken to the hospital, where she began the fight of her life. The problems began to pile up. Not only had Christle lost her only daughter, but she had suffered a head trauma from the accident. Against all odds, Christle proved to be a fighter. She learned to walk, breathe, and smile again. She pushed past the pile and walked down the aisle of adversity with a determination to take aim and flame!

Although Christle and her husband Steven began to seek out adoption, doors were not opening. Yet they still trusted God and kept a tight grip on His Word. They placed all their unanswered questions in the hands of the one who could handle them. Through the years of tears, Christle and Steven never stopped believing that God would restore. They never withdrew from the loyal view to trust in the Lord at all times.

Only God knows how many lives have been touched by Christle and Steven's aim to bring God fame. Then one day, God released that arrow that had been pulled back for a specific aim. With great force, the arrow landed exactly where God had intended, the birth of a beautiful miracle. Christle and Steven are now the proud parents of a precious son, Gabriel.

They are a model of a flame who believes in Jehovah Gmolah, the Lord of Recompenses.

There have been so many times when I wanted to give into my tale of woe, yet, when I focused on God's faithfulness, I pulled harder on my bow. What have you went through that has tried to force the withdrawal sign upon your flame? Satan has beaten so many black and blue with his corrupted view to doubt God's bigger picture. Friend, God is drawing you to share every realm of brokenness with Him.

I tell my daughters all the time, "Be real with Jesus. Share your cares, despairs, and those needed repairs. He can handle it!" When Satan begins to hiss, run to the total solace of God, "an ever-present help in trouble" (Ps 46:1). According to memorable-quotes.com, Helen Keller said it best, "Character cannot be developed in ease and quiet. Only through experience of trial and suffering can the soul be strengthened, ambition inspired, and success achieved."

Only God knows what pain flows from your past. Don't you settle for being an outcast. There is a new forecast for you. Mark 2:22 reminds us that God doesn't want us to put "new wine into old wineskins." Get rid of those old limited and inhibited thoughts. God wants you grinning about your new beginning.

Quit reliving the old, and start giving into the new you. Stop blaming, and start flaming. God is reliable so you must become pliable and be open to His dreams. When you allow God to fill any void, there really is a tremendous reward.

To be honest, I really want life to tickle, not put me in a pickle. But I have realized that, when life's pickle brings tears that trickle, it's really just a vehicle that transports you to a new opportunity. Trials allow room for God's work of an addition, recognition, ignition, submission, ammunition, and position. Let's look at these a little further.

ADDITION

Job was in a pickle that became a vehicle to an addition. The book of Job begins as a gripping drama of overwhelming trauma for a man who "feared God and shunned evil" (Job 1:1). At the beginning of this chapter, we learn that Job owned seven thousand sheep, three thousand camels, five hundred yoke of oxen, and five hundred donkeys. Like many of us, Job experienced the trial of a lifetime. However, Job 42 shows us that a faithful position results in faithful addition. Job 42:12 shows us that Job received "fourteen thousand sheep, six thousand camels, a thousand yoke of oxen and a thousand donkeys." As for his children, I believe that Job still got double. I believe the first ten were awaiting him in heaven. What started with plenty soon multiplied to twenty. Job's trials started as a clang of subtraction but ended in a bang of addition. I like God's math class. Don't you?

RECOGNITION

Shadrach, Meshach, and Abednego were in a pickle that became a vehicle for the recognition of a faithful God. These boys trusted God's way of deliverance in the midst of a hot spot. As a result, God received glory and honor. Daniel 3:28 tells us that Nebuchadnezzar said, "Praise be to the God of Shadrach, Meshach and Abednego." The Bible is filled with stories of people whose mess was stretched to a message of God's greatness. When the only son of a mother was raised back to life, people were "filled with awe and praised God" (Luke 7:16). Like the demon-possessed man, we need to come out of our pickle with an aim to run and tell others what Christ has done (Luke 8:39).

IGNITION

Daniel was in a pickle that became a vehicle for an ignition of holy fear and determination to seek God. As Daniel stayed persistent in his faith, God delivered him. As a result, a decree was issued for the people to "fear and reverence the God of Daniel" (Dan 6:26). Every trial is an entry point for God to create something new inside of you. God will use a bad situation to draw you to a new fire of faith, determination, and wisdom.

Don't despise what helps you become wise. Along with a holy fear, God can use the trial of the century to ignite a new revelation of who He is to you personally. Trials are an opportunity for God to give you the greatest miracle, Himself. Many times, we pray for God to ignite something new inside of our children, spouse, colleague, neighbor, family member, or even ourselves. Yet when a catastrophe strikes, we fall to pieces.

Like Paul, we often pray, "I want to know Christ," but we don't continue with that prayer that says, "And the fellowship of sharing in his sufferings" (Phil 3:10). We must wholeheartedly believe that God knows how to ignite something new even when we have a hazy view. Are you so in love with Christ that you are willing to bear on your body "the marks of Jesus" (Gal 6:17)?

SUBMISSION
Paul and Silas were in a pickle that became a vehicle for the submission of a family's soul to Christ. As Paul and Silas remained committed to the cause, the jailer and all his family were "filled with joy" and made the decision to "come to believe in God" (Acts 16:34). In addition, God used Mordecai and Esther's pickle to save a nation. How will you respond if God chooses to use your situation to help reach a lost soul? Will you cooperate with His wisdom? No matter what touches our lives, we are always on the winning side when we team up with God.

Trials will guide us to submit all things to Christ. High rising waters will force us to become God-sufficient, the character that makes God smile.

AMMUNITION
Paul's pickle of imprisonment gave us the ammunition of God's Word. While imprisoned, Paul wrote Ephesians, Philippians, Colossians, and Philemon. Paul's pickle of imprisonment is still affecting our lives today through the life-changing scriptures found in these books. Our struggles force us to the greatest medicine, the gospel of Jesus Christ. When you apply, the gospel will satisfy. With every trial, you come out with thunder and get your plunder when you learn to trust God and stand on His Word. God absolutely positively never makes a mistake. Your job is to just keep firing the ammunition of His Word.

POSITION
David had many pickles that became vehicles for the position of prayer and praise. Do you long to hear God speak of you as He said of King David in Acts 13:22? "I have found (insert your name) a man after my own heart; he will do everything I want him to do." Have you made up your mind that you will praise God at all times? David is the epitome of a man who lived with a zest because he learned to find rest in the midst of a storm. Throughout the stress, David was obsessed with praising God. Nothing could stop or crop his big heart of praise. David understood that prayer and praise must be paramount if you are to develop a deep friendship with God that sustains through life's tough times. Like David,

I have learned that a contender with praise is a container that is raised to a new level with Christ.

If we will cooperate with God, we will also see our pickle as a vehicle that allows us to see God in a new, fresh way. I don't know about you, but many times, I have wondered why some things in my life had God's approval for removal. But we must be determined to keep our candle lit with a feisty spirit even when we don't understand it. We must continually shout, "You are my God. My times are in your hands" (Ps 31:14-15). If you study the lives of the devoted in the Bible, you will see a pattern of approval for removal in some sort.

Abraham and Sarah were removed from their stay. Joseph was removed because he was in his brothers' way. Job's family, wealth, and health were all removed in one day. John was removed to an island far away. Daniel was removed because he chose to pray. Paul was removed because he would not stray. Stephen was removed because he chose one way, Jesus. And most importantly, Jesus was removed to be born in hay to pay our way.

Look Past the "Any" and See the "Many"

God truly understands that we are but dust and we are learning to trust His plans. I have come to this one conclusion about God. He is big enough to handle our whys when a home experiences the removal of a family member, friend, job, home, health, or any other thing we loved so dearly.

Sometimes, there simply aren't any answers raining down from heaven. At times, it seems that, when my flesh is involved in the greatest riot, all of heaven is extremely quiet. What do you do then? Don't seek an answer; seek the enhancer. Don't focus on an immediate reply; long for more of El Shaddai. Don't seek explanations; seek revelation from the Shepherd who has the best view of your valley and knows how you're going to tally all those blessings. Seek the one who can build you up and beautify the situation.

In order to take aim and flame, we must take our eyes off any (unanswered questions) and focus on the many (blessings to come). You must release all questions to the one who knows best.

When removal comes to my life in any size, shape, or form, I immediately begin to talk to myself. I say, "Tonya, this situation has already filtered through the Father's heart. Now, thrust your cares and trust your despairs on Him because He sees a "many." God will use you incredibly when you decide to trust and love Him, no matter what. You may not see the end results today, tomorrow, or perhaps even on this side, but you must choose to confide and abide in Christ and His sovereignty. God always responds to our prayers according to His great wisdom. Be confident in this. Your "any" and your "many" is connected to the harvest.

Abraham's any (unanswered questions) ushered him into becoming the father of many nations. Joseph's any kept many from starvation, including his own family. John's any gave us many insights with the book of Revelation. Paul's any gave us many books in the New Testament. Jesus's any gave many (the ones who would receive Him) an opportunity for eternal life. Mark 10:45 says, "For even the Son of Man did not come to be served, but to serve, and to give his life as a ransom for many." For what? Many!

God desires to help us understand that our any could minister to the many who have not accepted His invitation. "For many are invited, but few are chosen" (Matt 22:14). Some days, I say, "Lord, I don't have any energy to offer you today. I am empty. All I have are tears." However, as I focus on my aim to be His flame, I am reminded that He will transform my trial into triumph.

I must make up my mind, like the prophet Habakkuk did, and declare, "Though the fig tree does not bud and there are no grapes on the vines, though the olive crop fails and the fields produce no food, though there are no sheep in the pen and no cattle in the stalls, yet I will rejoice in the LORD, I will be joyful in God my Savior" (Hab 3:17-18).

The same God who put a laugh in the hyena can put a laugh in your arena of sadness. He can turn any situation around to gladness. After all, He has promised us in Psalm 30:5, "Weeping may stay for the night, but rejoicing comes in the morning."

During those times of unanswered questions, we must take our eyes off the strange and trust His long-range goal. Even through frustration, aggravation, and devastation, you can ignite a heart of passion. By all means, don't stop doing good. Be aware that Satan will always whisper, "It's just not worth it." When you're about to fall for that line, grab a hold of Galatians 6:9, "Let us not become weary in doing good, for at the proper time we will reap a harvest if we do not give up." And if your fire still needs some kerosene, turn to 1 Peter 4:19. "So then, those who suffer according to God's will should commit themselves to their faithful Creator and continue to do good."

One day, we will trade our list of any (unanswered questions) for many (rewards). We have a large duty that will result in the beauty of promotion. Brother Matthew told us so. One day, Jesus will say, "Well done, good and faithful servant! You have been faithful with a few things; I will put you in charge of many things. Come and share your master's happiness" (Matt 25: 23).

I challenge you to make it your habit to wake up every morning and say to Jesus, "Your name and renown are the desires of my heart" (Isa 26:8). Continually, I want to start my day saying, "Lord, I want to parent for Your glory, serve others for Your glory, write for Your glory, worship for your glory, study for Your glory, speak for Your glory, and live for Your glory in every way."

In order to take aim and flame, we need a clear vision of who we are apart from Christ. David put it best when he said, "You are my Lord, apart from you, I have no good thing" (Ps 16:2).

When you become saved, the Holy Spirit convicts you and draws you to a place of submission. However, the tender touch to surrender much does not stop there. The Spirit of God will draw you to a place where all you want to do is make God's name famous! The Spirit makes you more aware that it's not about you or even your view, but it's all about the true and faithful one, Jesus Christ.

We are here on this Earth to rely, apply, and testify about El Shaddai, the Almighty One. John 15:26 says, "When the Counselor comes, whom I will send to you from the Father, the Spirit of truth who goes out from the Father, he will testify about me. And you also must testify." Your conversations with the world are not about what you have done but rather what God's Son has done and how He gives you grace to run in this race.

I love what Paul said in 1 Corinthians 2:1-5:

> When I came to you, brothers, I did not come with eloquence or superior wisdom as I proclaimed to you the testimony about God. For I resolved to know nothing while I was with you except Jesus Christ and him crucified. I came to you in weakness and fear, and with much trembling. My message and

my preaching were not with wise and persuasive words, but with a demonstration of the Spirit's power, so that your faith might not rest on men's wisdom, but on God's power.

We must put away the presumption that we could ever function without the unction of the Holy Spirit. Allow the Lord to look deeply in your eyes as you hear Him whisper, "All your days were formed for My praise" (Isa 43:21).

Daily, we should aim to be a vibrant witness to His greatness. There is a gap in your map if you fail to tap into your purpose of bringing glory to His name. Our life's focus must be based upon the centrality of Jesus Christ. Paul put it best when he said in 1 Corinthians 15:31, "I die every day."

We have a mandate from our Father to go and share the good news of Jesus. In Acts 6, we see how Stephen set aim on his eternal home. His last words in Acts 7:56 capture his focus, "I see heaven." Precious flame, do you see heaven? Do you really see the view from heaven's perspective? May we grab a hold of heaven's view and brew with such tenacity to flame on like Stephen.

I can't say this enough. It is vitally important that we commune with the Holy Spirit. He will help us to get beyond ourselves and see that we are so unworthy yet graciously loved. John the Baptist pulled it all into perspective in John 1:27 as he spoke about Jesus. "He is the one who comes after me, the thongs of whose sandals I am not worthy to untie." What a privilege it is to be a part of His kingdom.

Be available. Be credible. Be versatile. Be adaptable. Be dependable. Be responsible. If we long to bring glory to God's name, we will hear the Master say one day," And glory has come to me through them" (John 17:10).

Like Mary, we must to learn to set aside good things for the best part, tapping into His heart. May we be a frame that will exclaim the words of Habukakah 3:2, "LORD, I have heard of your fame; I stand in awe of your deeds, O LORD. Renew them in our day, in our time make them known."

We must never forget that Satan would like nothing better than for us to search and perch on self-significance. My desire is to one day be able to echo the words to my Father that Jesus said, "I have brought you glory on earth by completing the work you gave me to do" (John 17: 4).

BIBLE STUDY IDEAS

CONNECT[10]
Play the Never Have I Ever Game. All participants must stand up. One group begins by saying something they have never done like, "Never have I ever been on a cruise." The participants who have done this must sit down. The last one standing is the winner and must begin a new game.

DIRECT
Share with your group a highlighted thought that ministers to you.

REFLECT
- Think back to the Ten Commandments. Which one reminds us that God does not share His glory?
- How can others see God's glory in our lives?
- How does our society try to steal God's story of glory?
- God can take any tragedy and turn it into triumph. What stories in the Bible are examples of how God took the "any" (problems) and replaced them with "many" blessings?
- Read John 11:1-6. Why did Jesus delay in responding to the news of Lazarus's sickness? What could be some reasons God may be delaying His answer to your plea?
- What "good" could God possibly bring from a bad situation? Try to discuss at least five things.

COLLECT
Research the following scriptures: 1 Chronicles 16:24, Romans 5:3, Romans 8:18, and 2 Corinthians 4:17-18. Take the time to read these with your group. Share your insight. How will these help us to flame on so God gets all the glory in our lives?

AFFECT

---

10   Idea from www.icebreakers.ws

Take the time to get with an accountability partner. Talk with your partner about a personal situation that has "many" questions but not "any" answers. Agree with your partner for "many" to replace the "any." Agree together for God to receive all the glory.

Praise is like sunlight to the human spirit:
we cannot flower and grow without it.

Jess Lair

───CHAPTER 8

Drawn to Exclaim

Her heart was weak, but her passion was unique. Her sweat was beading, but her faith was leading. Her voice was low, but her flame did glow. I stood by the bedside of my eighty-nine-year-old grandmother in the last few days of her life here on Earth. Although she had a small frame, she had a large exclaim. Congestive heart failure would not stop her teardrop or mountaintop praise for Jesus. She ministered to me to the highest degree when she spoke three specific words to me, "God is faithful." I had no idea that those three words would anchor me to such commitment during my own time of sickness.

With each new day, we have to remind ourselves, "The Lord is righteous in all his ways and loving toward all he has made" (Ps 145:17). From Genesis to Revelation, we continuously read how God was faithful to His people. Even though we fail Him, Jesus "will remain faithful, for he cannot disown himself" (2 Tim 2:13).

Despite our flaws, God remains faithful. Despite our claws, God remains faithful. Despite withdraws, God remains faithful.

WHAT BEAMS FROM YOUR LIFE

My flaming partner, when the word "faithful" becomes the theme of your life, it will beam from your life. Satan does not like a voice that loves to exclaim 2 Thessalonians 3:3, "But the Lord is faithful, and he will strengthen and protect you from the evil one." Satan doesn't like it when we "hold unswervingly to the hope we profess, for he who promised is faithful" (Heb 10:23). He doesn't like a voice of acclamation, but rather one filled with inflammation and too sore to speak about God's goodness.

Hear me, friend. Satan will fight you with spiritual laryngitis to the grave. Lucifer trembles at a vocal cord that is not afraid to use the sword (of the spirit). More than anything, I want my children to understand the power of exuberant and diligent praise. I pray the "praise of God be in their mouths and a double-edged sword in their hands" (Ps 149:6).

In Isaiah 43:21, God makes a point to share that we were created to declare His praises! We must live to formally, officially, and explicitly exclaim our love for Christ. God wants us to declare our excitement for His love. This probably sounds funny, but when I think of the word "declare," I think of a bear. I hear you chuckle. No, not just because it rhymes. Work with me here.

You see, a bear will make some noise when you get near hear his cub, grub, hub, or shrub. There is no taming a bear when she wants to declare her domain. A bear will cleave until you decide to leave her territory. She will exclaim to you, "Hey, Mister, I mean business here, so back off!" That's exactly how I picture a frame that is drawn to aim and flame for Christ. I want that "bear tenacity" in my praise.

We can't be passive about our praise. When the enemy gets in your territory, make some noise. When Satan comes around prowling, you get to growling. Don't just stand there. Open your mouth and declare. In Genesis 15:11, when the buzzards came to pursue, what did Abraham do? Yeah, he started to shoo! What about you?

God is looking for some Jeremiahs who will announce and arouse those who are spiritually asleep. If we fail to vociferate or speak out our faith, the enemy has a crack in the door to confiscate, devastate, dominate, separate, and strangulate your family's breath.

Jeremiah was a bear who tried to spare God's people from devastation by an exclamation of truth. This anointed prophet chose to express his aim for Christ over popular opinion and worldly success.

It's not a surprise to me that a flame never looks successful to the world. Jeremiah didn't attain material things or become very popular. He experienced rejection, disconnection, and objection for many years. Being thrown into prison and a cistern seems more like a big mess rather than a great success. However, I believe Jeremiah was one of the greatest achievers in all of history. For forty years, he was a flame who was compelled to exclaim God's words. He would not relent on his message to repent. He was a pioneer who learned to hear, fear, and cheer the words of the Lord. He was a vessel who learned to nestle in God. He allowed the Father to touch his mouth and plant His words inside his heart.

Jeremiah 2:2 is for you and me. We should be encouraged to "go and proclaim" to all those around us about the faithfulness of God. Jeremiah had a compassionate voice. So did John. Mark 1:3 tells us there was "a voice of one calling in the desert, 'Prepare the way for the Lord, make straight paths for him.'" Can unbelievers here you declare as you prepare for our Lord's returning?

As a flame, I lose all poise when it comes to making noise for Christ. Psalm 35:10 gets my daily, "Amen!" My whole being will exclaim, "Who is like you, O LORD?" Spiritual laryngitis is not going to cripple my voice from a steady rejoice. What about yours?

What Is the Theme of Your Life?

If I had to pick one big theme for my life, I think I would choose Philippians 4:4, "Rejoice in the Lord always, I will say it again: Rejoice!" I hope you are fully aware that Satan wants your voice of rejoice. He will use great force through the means of divorce, remorse, or any type of collision course to get it. He will play dirty with an ugly and sturdy grip. Satan wants your voice completely hoarse so you will not enforce any spiritual energy on another.

So how loud are you exclaiming your choice for Christ? Has your bellow become mellow? Do your habits still shout that you are sold out to Christ? Or maybe has something cut into your passionate discipline? I'm not the first to ask that question. The apostle Paul asked it many years ago in Galatians 5:7, "You were running a good race. Who cut in on you and kept you from obeying the truth?" Has a heave-ho or fatal blow caused your once-excited voice to go low, low, low?

Whatever your God-given task is, you are equipped to complete the work. But because you are equipped, the enemy wants you stripped from any energy to accomplish the task. We see this in the book of Ezra. When the captives from Judah returned from exile to rebuild the temple, God had equipped them to do the work. However, discouragement and fear were waiting to paralyze and terrorize what God had organized (Ezra 4:4-5).

As a flame, you must be aware that the enemy will disguise behind the word "neutralize." Being in a neutralized position is a lie from Satan. You are never standing still. You are either striving or depriving yourself from the joy of becoming more like Christ. If you remain neutral in your praise for God, beware! You are sure to get smacked, sidetracked, and ransacked by the enemy.

Just like the prophets Haggai and Zechariah, I want to encourage you to remember your purpose and complete the work. Keep yielding. Keep building. Keep shielding yourself from Satan's tug to get you to unplug from kingdom ministry.

I can attest to this. If the enemy gets your voice, he will get your source of strength. The serpent knows that "the joy of the Lord is your strength" against the wiles of the enemy (Neh 8:10). Every day, I choose to paint these words found in Psalm 119:175 upon my heart. "Let me live that I may praise you." If I neglect to paint, my voice will become faint.

Like vocal cords, our lives will lose their volume when we feel overused, irritated, or infected by a virus. A spiritual laryngitis is Satan's aim for every flame. Even when I am bone-tired, I must choose to praise Him. Don't allow Satan to get a wedge past your hedge of praise.

I still remember my grandmother's praise as the song "Amazing Grace" was sung to her during the last few days on this earth. With all her heart, my grandmother believed Jesus Christ offered everlasting life. How neat that God chose to take her home on what I call John 3:16. I can't think of any other day I would rather open my eyes to the sweet face of Jesus than the third month, sixteenth day. I'll never forget the last expression I saw upon my grandmother's face, a confident peace.

In every circumstance, God is speaking. Our job is to keep a steady grip instead of jumping ship. Therefore, we can experience how all things work "for the good of those who love him, who have been called according to his purpose" (Rom 8:28).

When God is working, we must stop jerking. When God is working, we must stop shirking. When God is working, we must stop smirking. His work requires teamwork. Our job is to keep praising and exclaiming, "He is faithful!"

If we are going to be a dedicated flock, we must trust His perfect time clock. Our heart's cry must be to magnify God's faithfulness at all times. John 7:38 says, "Whoever believes in me as the Scripture has said, streams of living water will flow from within him." I just can't help it. When I read this, my mind goes back to when my children were small and stood at the checkout line with me, needing to go the restroom. When water was about to flow, they needed to go! For goodness sake, they couldn't help but to exclaim that water was about to gush from their frames.

I guess that explains why I just can't keep still when I praise my Father. Now I know. The living water is trying to flow. I just can't contain it. When I am going through the Valley of Baca, which means "weeping," the Word tells me that I can make it a "place of springs" and go from "strength to strength" (Ps 84:6-7).

Through praise, I am connecting, and He is affecting all I am. Jeremiah exclaimed it best, "His word is in my heart like a fire, a fire shut up in my bones. I am weary of holding it in; indeed, I cannot" (Jer 20:9). Like Jeremiah, when you have experienced a touch from God, you don't care if you look odd. All you want to do is be a pod, a seed that can be spread abroad for the sake of Christ.

Don't you want to be a seed that is drawn to praise despite all the delays or dreaded x-rays? Life may have snapped some pictures of an unwanted "Wow!" but I'm determined to exclaim for my God anyhow. I will not give up my praise spot to a death pot of doubt! Elisha's servant taught me that in 2 Kings 4:38. Let's check out that story.

Elisha asked a servant to go out into the fields and gather some vegetables to put in a stew. Somehow, a poisonous vegetable or herb had gotten in the mix. The men began to cry out in 2 Kings 4:40, "There is death in the pot!" What did Elisha do? He got some flour and put it in the pot. What happened next? 2 Kings 4:41 tells us, "And there was nothing harmful in the pot."

Lesson learned: When it seems death is encroaching toward your pot, you must put something in that spot. And that something is praise that is sure to blaze and carry you through that momentary phase! Watch God raise your miracle from an empty tomb to a beautiful bloom.

Do a self-evaluation of your life right now. Where does God see "death in a pot" that needs a flowering spot of praise? Who are the people you know that the cravings and enslaving of the flesh are poisoning? Don't cower or become sour. Share the power of singing God's praise.

What an exciting opportunity we have been given to go and ask others to come to the feast (Matt 22:9). We must exclaim to others, "The wages of sin is death, but the gift of God is eternal life in Christ Jesus our Lord" (Rom 6:23). If you want to take aim and flame, you must exclaim to others, "There is death in sin's stew, but Jesus died for you!"

I understand what David longed for when he said, "My heart says of you, 'Seek his face! Your face, LORD, I will seek'" (Ps 27:8). Praise is not just a phase for me. It's a lifestyle.

According to Revelation, all of heaven is declaring. They are exclaiming, "Hallelujah! For our Lord God Almighty reigns. Let us rejoice and be glad and give him glory!" (Rev 19:6-7). I'm sold out on standing out for Christ. If I must make a spectacle of myself in my effort to spill my passionate love and gratitude to the one who loves me the most, then so be it.

One day, I was asking God to make me a greater exclamation mark for His glory. "I want to be a whole container of salt!" I cried. I began to comb over the scriptures in Colossians 1:10-12. I slowed right on down and began to meditate on the following scripture:

> And we pray this in order that you may live a live worthy of the Lord and may please him in every way; bearing fruit in every good word, growing in the knowledge of God, being strengthened with all power according to his glorious might so that you may have great endurance and patience, and joyfully giving thanks to the Father, who has qualified you to share in the inheritance of the saints in the kingdom of light.

All of a sudden, that scripture became alive. "That's it!" I cried. In order to be a whole container of salt, I need a pursuit. I need to bear fruit. I need a root. I need a suit. I need a boot. I need a hoot for Christ. Let's look at these closely.

PURSUIT

God wants you in hot pursuit to discover His very nature, His attributes, and His profound love so His flame will radiate from your life. Psalm 34:5 says, "Those who look to him are radiant." God wants us to have a fervent chase for Him so that, in life's ebb, we can still exclaim, "With your help I can advance against a troop; with my God I can scale a wall" (Ps 18:29).

Fruit

Your words will be mute if you fail to have fruit. People will tune out what you say if you do not display the attitude of Christ. God gets satisfaction when our love is demonstrated through action. Just as an apple is red, so are the words that Jesus said in Matthew 7:20, "Thus, by their fruit you will recognize them." Can people identify and verify the love of your Savior from your tree? Jesus tells us in John 15:4 that we won't be able to bear fruit unless we "remain" in Him. Before Christ can really use us to be a blessing, he must prune us by cutting back our branches. Sometimes, God shows me an area in my life that He desires to prune through my husband and children. I have always shared with them how they are all my accountability partners. I encourage them to share with me things they see in my life that aren't representing the attitude of Christ. Around our house, we number the fruit of the spirit. It is no surprise to hear my children say, "Mom, you sure do need some more of number nine (self-control)." Go ahead and laugh. You know you need some, too.

Root

If you take root downward, you'll bear fruit upward. We will exclaim the voice of the Lord when we are "like a tree planted by the streams of the water, which yields its fruit in season and whose leaf does not wither" (Ps 1:3). Have you ever noticed the branches on trees? They form the letter "y." Friend, your tree will often have many "whys" hanging from it. That is why we must have deep roots in the love of Christ. In the morning, I like to establish my roots in His love. I lift up my hands to form tree branches while my body represents the trunk of the tree. I form the letter "y" with the shape of my hands as I pray, "Father, before I meet any whys in my life today, I give you my Y of praise." I am convinced that God shares secrets with those whose roots of trust are in Him. When He does, we should exclaim the words of Mary, "May it be to me as you have said" (Luke 1:38).

Suit

If we are going to salt the earth, we must pay close attention to Colossians 3:12-14, which says to "clothe yourselves with compassion, kindness, humility, gentleness and patience . . . And over all these virtues put on love." If you want to be a fire, you must put on the attire to aim and flame. Ephesians 6:11-17 tells us to suit ourselves with the armor of God. Remember, we haven't been given any suit for the backside. Therefore, we should be confronting, not running from the enemy. The belt of truth, breastplate of righteousness, footgear to spread the Good News, shield of faith, helmet of salvation, and sword of the Spirit will always be the supernatural power needed to defeat the powers of darkness.

BOOT

When Jesus was tempted in the wilderness, He had a spiritual boot that positioned Him to stand on God's Word at all times. Don't you want God applauding your determination and declaring, "Now, that's one archer who shoots with flaming boots!" Our fiery boots will help us learn to stand for what is right. If you lean toward to the gray, you'll never get Goliath out of our way. Even if you have to stand alone, do it! You are building up your faith, which is vitally important. Just keep standing firm in your fiery boots, and God will fight your battle. In 2 Chronicles 20:17, God tells Jehoshaphat, "You will not have to fight this battle. Take up your positions; stand firm and see the deliverance the LORD will give you."

HOOT

We need to learn to hoot in the dim like an owl on a limb. Owls are amazing creatures to me. Did you know that owls aren't able to move their eyes all around? They keep their eyes focused on what is in front of them. Wow! If only we could do that. We need to quit looking back at Egypt and getting distracted. We need to make some noise for what is in our future. Once you experience the Father's touch on your life, you can't help but to be drawn to exclaim, "I will praise you, O LORD, with all my heart; I will tell of your wonders. I will be glad and rejoice in you; I will sing praise to your name, O Most High" (Ps 9:1-2). Praise is powerful arsenal.

Before leaving the scripture found in Colossians 1:10, I have to tell you what I found in my kitchen cabinet. I am holding a box of salt with a label that says 1 lb. 10 oz., the exact scripture number we just read. I just love when the Lord makes cool connections like that for me! It thrills me!

Is there anything that can come against your salt box and keep you from adoring in and pouring out? One day, I was reading Romans

4:18, where Paul was referring to the benefits of Abraham's faith, and I suddenly stopped after reading two words, "Against all—" Immediately, I began to exclaim to the Lord, "Against all sickness, against all sadness, against all loss, against all opposition, against all delays, against all frustrations, against all sufferings, against all unsuccessful surgeries, against all confused places, I choose to believe in You. I choose to believe in Your sweet Holy Spirit. I choose to believe in Your Word at all times."

As you continue to read this chapter in Romans, you will notice what Abraham became. I long for the day when God shows me all that became in my life because I chose to exclaim His beauty through the trials. His touch upon my life is so invigorating. Quite frankly, his touch is so refreshing and brisk that I'm truly willing to risk everything on His kingdom purposes.

Every day, we should exclaim, "Holy Spirit, help me to crucify this flesh." You see, your flesh will mess, stress, regress, and second-guess God's best for you. However, the Holy Spirit will nudge you to press toward life in Christ. John 6:63 says, "The Spirit gives life; the flesh counts for nothing." Your flesh will always magnify you. Your Spirit will always magnify God.

Before we close this chapter, let's look at just a few more characters in the Bible who were drawn to exclaim for Christ.

1. **Numbers 13-14: Caleb.** We can learn a lot from this man's unwavering and unfaltering exclaim of faith in God. Caleb's courage was secure in His loyal God. Caleb was a flame who was drawn to proclaim "we can certainly do it" (13:30). In Numbers 14:24, we see that Caleb had "a different spirit" who followed God "wholeheartedly." Therefore, Caleb got to flame onto the mountain he claimed.

2. **John 4: Woman of Samaria.** Here is a beautiful example of a woman who traded her water pot for a life-changing spot. When Jesus offered the Samaritan woman life-giving water, her life was forever changed. Although the woman saw her life as shame, Jesus had a bigger picture pinned by her flame. When the woman acknowledged the truth about Christ, she couldn't stop proclaiming the good news. As a result, "many of

the Samaritans from that town believed in him because of the woman's testimony" (verse 39). We must continually remind ourselves that we are surrounded by a harvest that needs us to proclaim the good news of Christ every day.

According to ministryinmotion.com, Lillian B. Yeomans once said, "Just believe what God says that Jesus has done for you . . . spirit, soul, and body—think about it, talk about it, sing about it, shout about it, and the praise cure has begun." My prayer is that you will be drawn to praise and raise your bow and arrow to aim and exclaim your love for Christ.

Bible Study Ideas

Connect[11]
Play the Who Am I Game. Each member should write down five famous people on a slip of paper and put them in a hat. If there are twenty people, there should be one hundred names in the hat. Now, get in a big circle and sit beside your prayer partner. If you have twenty people, then you will have ten teams. A hat with the famous names inside is passed around the whole circle for each person to pull out five names. Shhh! Don't tell anyone who your five famous people are. But, yes, you can laugh while you are wondering how in the world you are going to use only three words to describe that person to your partner. When the timer is started (you choose amount of time), each partner gets a chance to use three words to give his or her partner a clue of the famous person on his or her slip of paper while everyone else watches each group. It is the onlookers' job to keep an accurate score. When the timer goes off, all correct names will equal one point for that team. Then a new team begins the guessing game. The group that gets the most famous names correct is the winner.

Direct
Share with your group a highlighted thought that ministers to you.

---

[11]   Idea from www.icebreakers.ws

REFLECT
- How does praise affect your daily life?
- In Isaiah 63:3, Jesus said, "I have trodden the winepress alone." What are some examples of how we may have to trod alone in our "boot" with a "hoot" for Christ? What are the benefits?
- Your life exclaims something. Matthew 7:16 says, "By their fruit you will recognize them." How does your root affect your fruit?
- Draw a picture of a fruit that you want your life to resemble. Explain why you chose that fruit.
- Psalm 78:4 says that we should exclaim "the praiseworthy deeds of the LORD, his power, and the wonders he has done" to the next generation. What are some of your favorite ways to "exclaim" your praise for Christ?
- Read Psalm 118:1. Among your circle of Bible group friends, give an opportunity for any flame to exclaim a testimony of praise for all the good things Christ has done.

COLLECT
Research the following scriptures: Psalm 13:6, Psalm 28:7, Psalm 34:1, and Psalm 150. Take the time to read these with your group. Share your insight. How will these scriptures help us to flame on with praise?

AFFECT
Take the time to get with an accountability partner. Talk to your partner about how you feel when you exclaim God's praises. Pray together that God will show you new ways to proclaim His praise with greater boldness.

If I can stop one heart from breaking, I shall not live in vain;
if I can ease one life the aching, or cool one pain, or help one
fainting robin unto his nest again, I shall not live in vain.

Emily Dickinson

CHAPTER 9

Care for the Lame

Hmm, I'd really like to start this chapter a little different. So, I'm bringing out one of my poems to share.

> I watched a handicapped child at the park one day.
> He was watching his brother run, jump, and play.
> What caught my attention was when he would slap at his knee.
> He was overflowing with laughter and as happy as could be.
> Though sickness wouldn't permit him to get up out of his chair,
> His laughter for life could be heard everywhere.
> How in the world could he see this as a blessed event?
> Then the words of Paul hit me. He had learned to be content.
> While watching his brother skip, swing, and crawl,
> The smile on his face had a message for all.
> "Stop focusing on the things that may have been taken away.
> But rather be thankful for the breath God has given you today."
> Years later, when I faced a sickness that stole my run,
> I thought about that day and that precious little one.
> I thought about how the lad sat in his wheelchair in the sun.
> He got as close as he could to those having fun.
> Rejection of others could have caused him great wrath.
> But it was evident from his joy; he would not accept that path.
> This young boy forever imprinted my life that day
> Because he showed me the power of pushing "rejection" away.
> Every time that little buddy looked at me,
> His eyes seemed to say, "Ma'am, God has GREAT purpose for me!"

As long as I live, I'll never forget that little boy's face and his decision to embrace life's struggles with such a positive attitude.

A FLAME WILL CARE

For many years, I walked into my classroom every day with a lesson plan in my hand and God's love in my heart. During the last full year that I taught, the Lord prompted me to hang a sign in front of my classroom door with a picture of two children saying, "I have purpose! I'm so smart!" Before entering my door, my students would cheer this message. This sign became so contagious that even my principal would chuckle and cheer as he walked in.

Every child who entered my classroom felt welcomed, loved, appreciated, and excited about learning. My students were greatly influenced by the fact that someone really believed in them and their ability to soar in their learning. Now let's take that to a spiritual level. Does your heart hang a sign upon its door that says to others, "You have purpose"? Do those around you get a warm and fuzzy feeling because you share emotional healing found in Christ and Christ alone?

As a teacher, the changing point in my career was when I began to feel the heart of God every time I wrapped my arms around my students. You can't help but to look at others differently when you feel God's heart say, "I am concerned about their suffering" (Exod 3:7).

If I could pick one thought from this chapter that I want you to remember, it would be this. Every day, your contagious leap can greatly affect a broken-legged sheep. Through Jesus, we have the power to help change, rearrange, and exchange someone's poor self-image to know God's lineage of acceptance and love.

So how can we find the broken ones? Jesus tells us in Matthew 18:12 that our first step is to go and look for them. If you're seeking the flame that is blue, you're going to recognize those with a spiritual flu. People are spiritually coughing all around you. Like Philip in John 1:46, we should be drawing others to Jesus and encouraging them to "come and see" the one who can mend any broken leg. We must use our zest to help another to God's nest of love.

This world is filled with both big and little sheep that have lost their passionate leap. A cold avalanche of rejection has buried their hopes and dreams. They need your aim to love the lame. Mathew 24:12 says,

"Because of the increase of wickedness, the love of most will grow cold." But as ambassadors of Christ, our love must grow hotter.

How is this possible? We can make sure that our aim is "rooted and established in love" (Eph 3:17). Then we can become a branch to help others get up from the cold avalanche. In fact, Jesus himself called us a branch in John 15:5 when he said, "I am the vine; you are the branches." God wants our aim to branch out to the lame. God wants the light from our branches to shine brightly (Prov 13:9).

In Exodus 25:31-40, we are told that the lampstand in the tabernacle included branches that would hold light. I'm really starting to get this. God designed us to be a branch that would grow up, show up, and glow up to touch the lives of others. God's plan is that the "Branch of the LORD will be beautiful and glorious" (Isa 4:2).

I find it interesting that the tabernacle, ark, table, altar, and courtyard had specific measurements. But get this. The lampstand was not given any measurements. Likewise, as a flame, we can't put measurements on our light. We must be a bright witness to everyone around us. If I try to show favoritism toward those I choose to witness to, I am indeed trying to place a measurement on God's light. The Word plainly states in James 2:1, "Don't show favoritism." James 2:9 says, "But if you show favoritism, you sin and are convicted by the law as lawbreakers."

Jesus framed a great purpose for our flame in John 15:12, "My command is this: 'Love each other as I have loved you.'" Everywhere you steer, there are people who are near and want to hear your footgear coming to share the gospel of love.

A FLAME WILL SHARE

When you make up your mind to aim and flame, you will target your arrow to bring a leaf of belief toward others. Isn't that what the little dove did in Genesis 8? This bird provided a leaf of belief to what could have been overwhelming grief. Who wouldn't need a little spark in such a very noisy ark? I sure would!

In this story, we see how God sent His love by a little dove to minister to Noah. This dove reminded Noah that he would soon leave his tight space for a new embrace on life. That is exactly what we must be encouraging anyone who feels rejected to do.

When was the last time you offered a leaf of belief to a broken one? Once you start, the drive won't depart. It will become your life's mission. That's how I felt that cold winter day I left Walmart. Others passed this gentleman by as he sat out on the sidewalk with only a sigh. A homeless man. A broken one. I didn't know if he would listen to me, but I couldn't wait another moment to tell him how to break free. I'm sure he really wanted money. But I knew he really needed honey. Proverbs 24:14 tells us that wisdom is like honey. "If you find it, there is a future hope for you." So I opened the honey pot and poured and poured quite a lot.

I was so thrilled when this gentleman graced me the privilege to remind him that he had purpose. Much to my amazement, the gentleman smiled and responded. He continuously thanked me for taking the time to stop and remind him that God had a great purpose for his life.

I wonder how many people walk past the lame because their arrow does not have an aim. According to inspirationline.com, Sally Koch understood the power of helping others when she said, "Great opportunities to help others seldom come, but small ones surround us every day."

In Matthew 10:42, Jesus said, "And if anyone gives even a cup of cold water to one of these little ones because he is my disciple, I tell you the truth, he will certainly not lose his reward." Your encouraging cup can pull another one up. We must purposely find those who have been overlooked, overwhelmed, overcome, and undervalued and bring them to Christ. God is always revealing places that need His deep healing.

Let's be the one who realizes that we are "God's workmanship, created in Christ Jesus to do good works, which God prepared in advance for us to do" (Eph 2:10). Look around and see who needs to hear you say, "God has great purpose for your life today!"

Be willing to do something extraordinary for another. Aim your flame to serve. Place a high priority on encouraging others.

The title of comforter translates to the word, "paraklete," which means "to encourage." If we submit our arrow in His hands, God will aim toward "the poor, the crippled, the lame, the blind" so we can invite them to the table of the Lord (Luke 14:13).

Our voices should be crying out, "Lord, give me your compassions!" so we can see miracles take place. Mark 1:41 says, "Filled with compassion, Jesus reached out his hand and touched the man."

We should set our aim to be generous toward those in need. Generosity is God's pleasure and gets blessed full measure. "Give, and it will be given to you. A good measure, pressed down, shaken together and running over, will be poured into your lap. For with the measure you use, it will be measured to you" (Luke 6:38).

When we set our aim toward the lame, we will truly care about those drowning in the waters of rejection. We must pay attention to the cue and run to their rescue.

A Flame Takes Another Up for Air

When others receive a bad report, do you swim over with great support? Do you lend an ear and help others to the pier of healing? Speaking of swimming, did you know that a mother dolphin understands the power of helping a sick baby dolphin? The mother will swim to the rescue and support the sick dolphin to the surface so it can breathe fresh air. But what about us? Do we even notice that many people around us are being "tossed back and forth by the waves and blown here and there by every wind of teaching and by the cunning and craftiness of men in their deceitful scheming" (Eph 4:14)?

As the body of Christ, we should be compelled to swim out and help. If we are gossiping about a brother or sister dolphin who has managed to get caught in a net of sexual immorality, drunkenness, rage, impurity, greed, debauchery, lust, impurity, or idolatry, we are sadly disconnected from the heart of God. When a family member or colleague is caught in a sinful act, how do you react? The world will surround him or her with a laughing racket, but we must throw him or her a spiritual life jacket. Don't beat him or her up. Heat up his or her life with a flame of encouragement.

What do you do when you see people at the grocery store or the mall who seem to have no joy? If you really love your Lord, you will not dodge to avoid them. If you are a flame with an aim, you will go after them. Hug her neck. Shake his hand. Get with God's plan. Let them feel God's love flowing from your flame. Be inconvenienced for a soul that needs to be told, "You have great purpose!" Galatians 6:10 says, "As we have opportunity, let us do good to all people." You can't pray, "Lord use me," if you aren't willing to open your eyes to God's opportunity.

Many times, the problem is that we do not want to be interrupted or inconvenienced. Thank goodness, mother dolphins don't respond that way. When a baby dolphin is born, a mother dolphin must inconvenience herself by swimming on her side so she can nurse the new calf.[12]

When was the last time you encouraged a babe in Christ? Proverbs 12:25 says, "An anxious heart weighs a man down, but a kind word cheers him up." We are choosing a delay when we opt to say, "If there is anything I can do for you, just let me know." Hello! You can do something. Put your love into action. Take the time to lend them your ear. Pray and ask God to show you how to specifically help those in need.

Many have the attitude, "That situation is just too messy for me to get involved in. I'm sorry. I just don't do blood." Thank goodness the Samaritan was willing to handle blood. Luke 10:34 tells us that the Samaritan went to the one who others passed by and "bandaged his wounds, pouring on oil and wine" (Luke 10:34). There are many wounds out there that God can use our hands to swathe in His love. As we spend time with Jesus, we will develop an ear that will "hear the voice of the Lord saying, 'Whom shall I send?'" (Isa 6:8). Will your reply be, "Here am I! Send me!"

Some people won't do blood. Other people won't do mud. They don't want to get dirty. Thank goodness the friends in Mark 2:4 didn't feel that way. They were determined to get their paralyzed friend to Jesus. Are you that determined to see your friend bud even if it requires dealing with mud?

When you've experienced your own flop yet felt the touch of the Master's prop, nothing will stop you from getting someone else to the hilltop, not even a storm. Let's embark on a story found in Mark that I love to read about. In Mark 4:35-41, Jesus initiates the rescue with his crew in the little canoe (actually a boat). His rescue was to pursue a sick dolphin with many demons. Jesus Christ cared so much that he would fight a storm to pursue God's plan to save just one man.

The key word in this story is mercy, which is found in Mark 5:19, "Go home to your family and tell them how much the LORD has done for you, and how he has had mercy on you." Oh, wow! Mercy makes all

---

12   Angela Atkinson, "How do Dolphins Take Care of their Young?" http://www. ehow.com/how-does_4566867_dolphins-care-their-young.html

the difference. When you think about all the Lord has done for you on a daily basis, you are always looking to tell someone about God's amazing grace and mercy.

In Matthew 5:7, Jesus said, "Blessed are the merciful, for they will be shown mercy." Every time you show mercy, your character is strengthened and lengthened. Micah 6:8 says that God requires us to love mercy.

We should never forget that God has called us to be fishers of men. I don't want to stand before Jesus with great regret because I have an empty net. Like Peter, I want to launch out into the deep and catch a heap of fish. Isaiah 42: 6 says, "I will keep you and will make you to be a covenant for the people and a light for the Gentiles." Again, I ask: Who is God calling you to be a light for?

Before we close this chapter, I want us to look at some people in the Bible who cared for the lame.

1. **Acts 9:36-42: Dorcas.** This remarkable woman stands out for her love and care for needy. The Bible says she was "always doing good and helping the poor" (Acts 9:36). This woman used the gifts God had given to her to dispense blessings to the disadvantaged. Dorcas should inspire all of us to impact our family, church, community, and nation with acts of kindness to encourage others to flame on.

2. **2 Samuel 9: David.** In 2 Samuel, we see how David showed compassion to a man named Mephibosheth who must have felt that no one cared for his soul. Crippled by a fall at the age of five, Mephibosheth must have often wondered, "Why am I still alive?" However, God had purpose for Mephibosheth, just like he has purpose for you and me. I am convinced that a flame must seek out those people who felt like David did in Psalm 142:4, "No one is concerned for me. I have no refuge; no one cares for my life." People who feel this way surround us. David is a great example of a flame who wanted to be a kindness dispenser. Sin once marred and scarred us, but God looked deep within and saw the flame inside of us. We must do the same for others.

If you want God's hands moving in your area, use your hands to remove another's barrier. God has called us to "live as children of light" (Eph 5:8). Every one of us has been called to the "seed ministry." We must *proceed* with love. We must *exceed* with love. We must *intercede* with love. Then we will *succeed* with love. Be a flame that seeks out the lame. Then we may hear someone say to us the words found in Philemon 1:7, "Your love has given me great joy and encouragement, because you, brother, have refreshed the hearts of the saints."

BIBLE STUDY IDEAS

CONNECT
Play the Letter Game, much like Scattergories. The group leader should have made a list of biblical categories such as Bible boy name, Bible girl name, Bible animal, Bible city, and so forth. Place dominant letters of the alphabet in a box that would be easy to connect a Bible word with. Have a member pull out a letter. Each participant is given two minutes to record a word that begins with that letter on his or her card. If someone else has the same word as you do, you must scratch that name out. One point is earned for each word you come up with. The person with the most points at the end of the game wins. Play a few times with different letters.

DIRECT
Share with your group a highlighted thought that ministers to you.

REFLECT
- Think about the last encounter that you had with a broken one. What kinds of things did you say or do to encourage him or her?
- Who were some of the broken ones that Jesus ministered to?
- How did His touch affect their lives and change their route? Be specific.
- Read Psalm 41:1. Can you share a personal example of this?
- What are the top three fruits of the spirit that you feel are vitally important to minister to broken people? Explain why.
- How can we better train our children to seek out broken ones at school?

- If you were ministering to a broken one and he was to ask you what was so great about your God, what would you say?
- Which group of people has God given you a tremendous passion to minister to, for example, young children, teenagers, cancer victims, divorced parents, and so forth? Why do you feel connected to them?

COLLECT

Research the following scriptures: Proverbs 12:18, John 13:35, Hebrews 6:10, and 1 John 4:11-12. Take the time to read these with your group. Share your insight. How will these help you to focus on being a flame that cares for the lame?

AFFECT

Take the time to get with an accountability partner. Without mentioning any names, share a prayer request for a broken one. In unity, pray that these people will realize they have great purpose.

God proved His love on the Cross. When Christ hung, and bled, and died, it was God saying to the world, "I love you."

Billy Graham

——CHAPTER 10

Why He Came

Why did He do it? What in the world made Jesus surrender and leave His heavenly splendor?

Heaven's loss was all about a cross. Jesus would travel a lonely path filled with enemies of wrath. Heaven's heartrending view was about a rescue. Yours. Mine. Jesus came with one aim, to give His life as a ransom for our shame. God came for our flame to experience fullness! Not just in heaven but right here on Earth.

As you flip the pages of this chapter, may you be reminded that you are God's jewel created for a full, abundant life. God has designed you for replete, not defeat. God has great intentions for you that are chock-full and filled with bounteous and bursting-to-the-brim experiences. Jesus was very specific about the word "full" in John 10:10 when He said, "I have come that they might have life; and have it to the full."

My goal in this chapter is to pull and pull the word full, full, full to the focus of your life. I pray that anyone reading this chapter who might have a "barely get by" fatigue will join the Big League of Fullness.

Start seeing yourself with more, and I mean GALORE. Jesus came for your flame's abundance. God wants you living at your full potential. Your past or even present circumstances do not limit the greatness that God anxiously desires to pour into you. Look past the disaster, and open up your alabaster box of worship unto God.

According to Psalm 8:5, God has crowned us with "glory and honor." God has given us the opportunity to be planted in Him so that whatever we do will prosper (Ps 1:3). You don't have to settle for the trash dump or little stump mentality. You can be a tree that nourishes and flourishes with overflow. Fullness should be the aim and claim of every wannabe blue flame. Jesus is our model of fullness. Let's take a look at His example.

COMPASSION

Our God is full of compassion. In Psalm 116:5, we learn, "The Lord is gracious and righteous; our God is full of compassion." James 5:11 tells us, "The Lord is full of compassion and mercy." As we learn to live fully compassionate lives and offer such mercy to others, we will learn how to respond like Christ. When a driver pulls out in front of me and I have to slam on brakes to keep from hitting him, I'm not feeling that "fullness of compassion" moment. Are you with me? My flesh wants to bear down on the horn as I scream, "What in the world are you doing?" However, it never fails. I look over to my children who are watching my every reaction. All of a sudden, the word "fullness" will come floating across my brain. Then I picture what Christ would do. He would give that driver a cup full of mercy. Then He would praise God for protection at that intersection.

UNFAILING LOVE

Our God is full of unfailing love. In Psalm 33:5, we learn, "The LORD loves righteousness and justice; the earth is full of his unfailing love." I like to start my day off by meditating on 1 Corinthians 13. I want to be a frame that is drawn to flame, "Love is patient, love is kind. It does not envy, it does not boast, it is not proud. It is not rude, it is not self-seeking, it is not easily angered, it keeps no record of wrongs. Love does not delight in evil but rejoices with the truth." I've come to realize that we must deal with a selfish intent that tries to keep our love from being patient. It takes a "set aim and flame" desire to attack our cruel mind that keeps us from being kind. It takes zeal to keep our cruel words subdued. Therefore, our love won't come across as rude. I pray that God will increase my understanding of what His love really looks like. God can't bless a tight fist that continues to resist His prompting to love others. As you find yourself loving more, you will find yourself giving more. John 3:16 says, "God so loved that He gave." At the point of a difficult decision, ask yourself, "Which choice prompts me to display unfailing love that gives unto others?" When we make the right choice, it will force us to become a stronger vessel that is drawn to take aim with purpose.

JOY

Our God is full of joy. In Luke 10:21, we learn that Jesus was "full of joy through the Holy Spirit." Jesus wants us to live with a fullness of joy that will employ us for great ministry. At the most difficult times in our lives, we must set joy before us in order to take aim and flame. Christ is our example. Hebrews 12:2 says, "Who for the joy set before him endured the cross." Before going to the cross, Jesus prayed about our joy. He prayed we would have "the full measure" of His joy within us (John 17:13). May God help us to yield completely to the work of the Holy Spirit so we can walk in that fullness of joy available to us daily.

GRACE AND TRUTH

In John 1:14, the Word tells us that Jesus was "full of grace and truth." God wants to free us from our past and point us to His grace and truth. As a flame, we can't afford to cling to past failures. We are reminded in Romans 8:1, "Therefore, there is now no condemnation for those who are in Christ Jesus, because through Christ Jesus the law of the Spirit of life set me free from the law of sin and death." When the enemy tries to steal our fullness, we must apply the weapon of grace and truth. In addition, we must be ready to stand guard against any idols that come to rob us of fullness. Idols are a counterfeit that will cause you to "forfeit the grace" that Jesus offers to all His people (Jon 2:8). God's vision for our lives is a fullness of unmerited favor and truth. God desires that your daily conversations be "full of grace, seasoned with salt, so that you may know how to answer everyone" (Col 4:6).

REWARDS

Our God is full of rewards. 2 John 1:8 encourages us to be careful in our living so we "may be rewarded fully." Christ came to fully reward those who "earnestly seek Him" (Heb 11:6). As a teacher and parent, I love to give my children and students rewards. And so does Christ. More and more, we should be asking Christ which areas in our lives we have ignored that needs His help to change. What attitudes are keeping us from the rewards God has for us?

As we come to understand the heart of Christ and what He came to give us, we will live to flame on with fullness. Like Abraham, we can be "fully persuaded" that God will keep his promises of total abundance in our lives (Rom 4:21). We must be on guard for the traps that give a scare and still our air. Just like potholes. Believe me. If there is a pothole in the road, my car will find it. I don't know what it is about potholes and me. I just don't straddle them right or something. Just like those aggravating potholes, Satan has an assignment to remove your position out of alignment. He doesn't want us to experience the fullness of the ride on the safe side. He wants us to collide with the weak that will give us a leak. As a flame, we can become more aware of the traps that steal our air. After all, the Word warns us that Satan "comes only to steal and kill and destroy" (John 10:10).

As we study the scriptures, we can find other ways in which we can be drawn to fullness. Let's take a look at some of these.

Fully Obedient

Exodus 19:5 says, "Now if you obey me fully and keep my covenant, then out of all nations you will be my treasured possession." As our heart becomes soft and pliable to living God's standards, it will become a consuming blaze for Christ. A casual attitude about obedience signifies a lack of understanding about God and a lack of love for God. Spending time in the secret place with God and allowing Him to rub his very nature on us will help us fight the disease of compromise.

Fully Committed

1 Kings 8:61 says, "But your hearts must be fully committed to the LORD our God, to live by his decrees and obey his commands." King Asa was an effective king because he was "fully committed to the LORD all his life" (1 Kgs 15:14). However, Solomon came to the end of his life feeling meaningless because "his heart was not fully devoted to the LORD his God" (1 Kgs 11:4). Let us not forget that Paul encourages us in 1 Corinthians 15:58 to be fully committed to the work of the Lord. "Let nothing move you. Always give yourselves fully to the work of the Lord, because you know that your labor in the Lord is not in vain."

FULL OF LIGHT
Matthew 6:22 reminds us of our destiny for the fullness of light. "If your eyes are good, your whole body will be full of light." Like my favorite reptile, Mr. Turtle, you must have good eyesight. You must "look straight ahead" and "fix your gaze directly before you" (Prov 4:25). When we walk into our place of work, we can "come in the full measure of the blessing of Christ" (Rom 15:29). Then God will be glorified through us.

FULLY ARMED
Ephesians 6:11 tells us to "put on the full armor of God so that you can take your stand against the devil's schemes." We have three enemies: the devil, our flesh, and the world. We must be ready to protect ourselves against the blows from each one of these foes. The stakes are too high to ever deny that we need God's fullness of strength to help us. Luke 11:21-22 tells us that "when a strong man, fully armed, guards his own house, his possessions are safe. But when someone stronger attacks and overpowers him, he takes away the armor in which the man trusted and divides up the spoils." There's no alarm when you are fully armed.

FULL OF UNDERSTANDING
God desires for us to walk in understanding. In Colossians 2:2, we see this vision in Paul as he desired to see others "encouraged in heart and united in love, so that they may have the full riches of complete understanding, in order that they may know the mystery of God, namely, Christ." As we become more intimate with the Father, the Son, and the Holy Spirit, we can have the blessings of Naphtali, who was "abounding with the favor of the LORD" and also "full of his blessing" (Deut 33:23).

FULL OF THE WORD
God wants us to know His Word so we can recognize strongholds that try to paralyze our ability to move forward in Christ. How can we "take captive every thought to make it obedient to Christ" if we do not know the Word (2 Cor 10:5)? Like Paul, may we be able to share "the word of God in its fullness" (Col 1:25).

If we choose to forfeit the fullness of obedience, commitment, light, armor, understanding, and the Word, we are opening our lives to "become filled with every kind of wickedness, evil, greed and depravity" and to be "full of envy, murder, strife, deceit and malice" (Rom 1:29). So many people live short of the affluent life God has planned for them because "their mouths are full of cursing and bitterness" (Rom 3:14). I am convinced that Christ desires you to become "active in sharing your faith, so that you will have a full understanding of every good thing in Christ" (Phlm 1:6). Christ came for your completeness.

Many characters in the Bible exemplify a desire for the fullness of Christ. Let's look at these:

1. **Ephesians 3:19: Paul.** I just love reading about the apostle Paul. In this chapter, he encourages you to "know this love that surpasses knowledge—that you may be filled to the measure of all the fullness of God." Just as Paul carried the Gospel across the Roman Empire, God wants us to carry the gospel across the world with fire. Paul was so satiated with a love for Christ that his fullness always encouraged him to flame on and say, "The Lord's will be done" (Acts 21:14). When you are bursting with a desire for more of Christ, you can't help but to be a heart-stirring mouthpiece for God.

2. **Mark 14:1-9; Luke 10:38-42: Mary of Bethany.** Mary is a beautiful example of a person with a spiritual hunger for the fullness of knowledge that Christ has to offer each and every one of us. Not only did she sit at Christ's feet, she worshipped at His feet and anointed His feet with her best. What posture did Mary take on to do these things? We don't often think of fullness associated with this word, but Mary shows us the power of silence. If we really want to experience the fullness of Christ, we must set aside time for the "best part" and be silent to hear His voice. The enemy will do all he can to keep us busy and burdened so we won't choose to "be still before the Lord and wait patiently for Him" (Ps 37:7). When you learn to sit, you reap the benefit. When you learn to be still, you'll experience great fullness in His will as you flame on.

I firmly believe the manifestation of wisdom, knowledge, faith, and all the other gifts discussed in 1 Corinthians 12:7-11 are all intended to be used to serve the whole body and encourage us to a greater fullness in Christ. Prayer plays such a part in experiencing this fullness of life. During those getaway moments with God, He can influence your mind to want His desires for your life. When you pray, begin to think monumental. Blink instrumental. May you become tickled pink with transcendental expectations of what God can do in your life. Through prayer, we learn to kink and shrink the small view of what God can do with a vigilant spirit.

In addition, setting your aim on being thankful and grateful will fan your flame to fullness. Narcissism is a rock that blocks fullness. If I choose to always think of me, I have a life guarantee of a joy killer. Like salt poured on an icy road, words of gratitude force the frozen to thaw out and melt away. It is so much healthier to focus on your bliss instead of what you have missed. According to photoquoto.com, Jim Stovall said, "In those times we yearn to have more in our lives, we should dwell on the things we already have. In doing so, we will often find that our lives are already full to overflowing." An epidemic of ungratefulness has peppered the lives of many. Don't let it find itself on your plate. Nothing can hinder the abundance of your uniqueness but you. Jesus came to pay your lease for an increase to fullness. When your eyes see a mess, God sees success and fullness for those who put their trust in Him.

BIBLE STUDY IDEAS

CONNECT[13]
Play the Birthday Game. Participants are divided into two groups where they will form a straight line. Now, they must arrange the line by birthdays starting with January to December. However, they must communicate this without talking or writing anything down. When the group is ready, the leader goes down the line to let each member announce his or her birthday. The most accurate team is the winner. Remember, absolutely no talking!

DIRECT
Share with your group a highlighted thought that ministers to you.

---

[13] www.traininggames.com

REFLECT
- How would you respond if someone were to ask you the following question: How can I experience true fullness on this earth?
- Christ came that we could have "life abundantly." What does that mean to you?
- What are some personal things in your life that you are doing to draw closer to the fullness of God?
- As a Christian, what kinds of things distract us from the "fullness of God"?
- Job 42:17 tells us that Job died "full of years." What is your picture of a life that is "full of years" spiritually?
- Read Acts 6: 3-5, 7:55. What was Stephen "full of"? How did this effect his devotion to Christ?

COLLECT
Research the following scriptures: Psalm 16:11, John 1:16, Ephesians 1:22-23, and Colossians 2:9-10. Take the time to read these with your group. Share your insight. How will these help you to focus on the fullness that Christ came to give you?

AFFECT
Take the time to get with an accountability partner. Talk about how your "focus" affects "fullness." Pray for your partner to experience the "abundant life."

Faith is a living and unshakable confidence, a belief in God so assured that a man would die a thousand deaths for its sake.

Martin Luther

────CHAPTER 11────

Faith's Hall of Fame

You may be one of those who have an incredible gift with sports. If so, be very thankful. I could never get that dribbling thing down pat, nor could I get good timing with a ball and bat. My hands just aren't coordinated for any type of ball game so my chances of being in the Hall of Fame are pretty slim to none. Therefore, I have chosen to set my eyes on Faith's Hall of Fame. So, teammate, let's put on our running shoes and head for the book of Hebrews. Let's discuss the importance of being drawn to a new level of faith.

I am not interested in seeing my name on an earthly plaque. My eyes are focused toward the flaming faith track. This flame has set her aim on passing a baton of faith to the next generation. I want my lips to constantly be encouraging others to "have faith in God" (Mark 11:22). Just like Enoch. Just like Noah. Just like Abraham. Oooh! Let's stop here a minute and talk a little bit more about Abraham, a man of unwavering faith.

To the natural mind, God's promise to Abraham to have a son seemed impossible. I just love how God used Mr. One Hundred Plus to surprise all of us! Likewise, God wants to use your life to surprise others about what He can do with extreme faith. My heart's desire is to hear the Master say, "Your faith in God has become known everywhere" (1 Thess 1:8).

EXERCISE YOUR FAITH SHAKER

In Hebrews 11:8-12, the scriptures tell us that Abraham was called to go to a new place. Abraham never said, "God, if you show, then I'll go."

Abraham simply became an immediate responder of great faith who was willing to give up customary for the extraordinary. Abraham sprinkled his faith shaker and carried out God's will all the way. He never stopped halfway. He kept pushing the pedal and refused to settle for anything less than what God wanted him to do. What if Abraham's father had done that?

Genesis 11:31 tells us that Abraham's father, Terah, took his family and set out for Canaan. However, "when they came to Haran, they settled there." That's exactly what the enemy wants you and me to do, settle and not pedal.

Oh, did we have to go here? Yes, we did. I'm going to meddle because I don't want you to settle for mediocre. I don't want you to stop halfway. I want you to have extreme faith! I want your faith to perk for that good work that God is going to complete in you (Phil 1:6).

God ideas require faith, but don't worry. God has got your back on this faith track. Whatever it is that God has showed you, keep moving toward it. Keep your foot to the pedal and your eyes on the medal of great faith.

Opposition may produce a pause, but extreme faith gets God's applause. The enemy hates your faith in Christ. He is always looking for a moment to trade your faith with His fear. Satan has often tricked many people to fall for the exchange when life brings a new change. When we move from health to sickness or job to unemployment, we have to shake faith out of our lives like never before. Hold on tight with all your might.

Like Abraham, you and I must have great confidence in our barrier-breaking God. Abraham didn't reason. He chose to season his thoughts with a faith shaker. He chose to ignite a trust that refused to let go of God's promises. Your situation may look like death, but sprinkling faith brings God's breath that will resurrect that promise to life.

Without a match, a candle can't be lit. Without a latch, your get-up-and-go will quit. Therefore, we must latch on to God with steadfast faith.

Faith That Brings a Smile to Your Maker

What kind of faith makes God smile? I believe it's a faith that is always drawn to be . . .

FIRM

Isaiah 7:9 says, "If you do not stand firm in your faith, you will not stand at all." You know you are being drawn to take aim and flame with great faith when you have no options left, yet you still choose to say, "Yep, it's going to happen! Just you wait and see!" We will never become familiar with the Hall of Faith until we deliberately decide that we will not "waver through unbelief" (Rom 4:20). Faith is climbing the arduous hill, no matter what you see or feel. Firm faith is a disciplined faith. When bad news arrives, extreme faith doesn't start turning but keeps reaffirming, "I serve a faithful God!"

ACTIVE

In Philemon 1:6, Paul encourages you to "be active in sharing your faith." Active faith fights against the tide and refuses to divide to the popular side. It is not dinky or slinky. This kind of faith will spill over into everything we say and do. This kind of faith looks every day for people in your path that you can spray with the love of Christ. When your faith is active, it doesn't mind being inconvenienced or interrupted for a chance to share the kingdom news. We have been commissioned. There's no excuse. Go ahead and induce. Give birth to extreme faith and watch God use you to introduce others to Christ.

IMPACTING

In Matthew 17:20-21, Jesus encourages that you can have such impacting faith that "nothing will be impossible for you." Your faith has the power to force you over the hurdle and supply a fertile place in which God can position a growing promise. So many people get discouraged when they can't see their promises being fulfilled in their timing. Our faith can spark their lives and empower them to keep on believing in God for every promise. We should be stirring up the gift inside others with this insightful word, "The promise comes by faith" (Rom 4:16). We can empower people with enduring faith to hold on to their expectations. Paul longed to see his brothers in Christ so they would be "mutually encouraged by each other's faith" (Rom 1:11-12). Be active about impacting others with great faith.

TENACIOUS

In Matthew 15:21-28, a Canaanite woman teaches us the effects of faith that is packed with tenacity. Jesus responds to her faith with such approval: "Woman, you have great faith. Your request is granted." Like Benadryl, your faith will spill and go to work when it's applied to any itchy, irritated area of fear. God loves it when we cry out in faith and say, "Lord, the battle is yours! There is no way I will see positive results without Your divine intervention."

HOPEFUL

Hebrews 11:1 teaches us that faith always hopes. Faith looks straight in the face of challenges and answers, "I am absolutely sure. I am absolutely certain that my God is going to see me through this thing." One of my favorite scriptures is found in Psalm 71:14, "But as for me, I will always have hope; I will praise you more and more." We can always be hopeful no matter what limitations arise. God is our constant help.

You know you have set aim to flame when you can look back at difficult situations and see that your faith led through the dead, past the dread, into the red target. You must remain confident that God will absolutely "repay you for the years the locust have eaten . . . and you will praise the name of the LORD your God, who has worked wonders for you" (Joel 2:25-26).

When life hits you the hardest, rise up and cry out, "I'm remaining with sustaining faith!" Keep beating that faith drum for the best is yet to come. Stir up your zest and pass that test so God can promote you to a new level of conquest.

Your faith is crucial to your witnessing flame. Let's look at the benefits of faith.

FAITH FIGHTS

1 Timothy 6:12 says, "Fight the good fight of faith." How encouraging it is to know that our faith will fight every snakebite, dark night, and treacherous plight that we face. 2 Corinthians 1:24 says that "it is by faith you stand firm." Choose faith's team and watch God's victory beam. As a flame, we must know that our faith can't "rest on men's wisdom, but on God's power" (1 Cor 2:5).

FAITH LIGHTS

Your faith will light the way for others to receive spiritual, emotional, and physical healing. Hall of Faith people are driven to find others who need faith to light their way to the voice that says, "Take heart, son; your sins are forgiven" (Matt 9:1). There are times when darkness is challenging your brother's faith. Step up to the plate and allow God to use your faith to shine hope all around him.

FAITH WRITES

Stories about characters such as Shadrach, Meshach, and Abednego inspire us. God desires to write even more books of the Bible from your life as you allow your faith to exclaim His faithfulness. Paul shares with the Roman Christians how their faith was "being reported all over the world" (Rom 1:8). Is your faith unraveling, or is it traveling to a greater distance? There's no doubt about it. As your "faith continues to grow," your outreach will "greatly expand" (2 Cor 10:15).

FAITH IGNITES

Faith ignites fiery answers to your prayers. In Matthew 9:29, Jesus said to the blind man, "According to your faith will it be done to you." Although some healing is instant where others are a process, faith is crucial. Sharing God's Word is an excellent way of igniting faith in others. Romans 10:17 says, "Consequently, faith comes from hearing the message, and the message is heard through the word of Christ." I love to surround my home with encouraging scripture of faith.

FAITH INVITES

Your faith invites the love of Jesus to go to work in all areas of your life. Galatians 5:6 says that faith expresses "itself through love." If you want to monitor your faith, evaluate your love for others. Faith invites the sweet Holy Spirit to activate, navigate, and exhilarate God's power in our lives.

WHAT FLAMING FAITH SAYS

Whether you realize or not, your faith has a voice. It says to God:

- **"I will hold to your promise."** Many times, we get a leak in our faith when God doesn't seem to be on our personal timetable. Faith says, "I'm going to outlive and outlast any thought that tries to persuade me that God doesn't have my best interest in mind at all times." The enemy and our flesh fight us with thoughts such as: "If God was so faithful, He wouldn't have allowed this to happen to me. If God really loved me, He would do something now." We must realize that this will paralyze our flame if we don't learn to aim with abiding faith that says, "I am going to cling to my faith in Christ. I am going to wear out the doubt with a shout of faith." Enduring faith will respond to any discouraging thought with this scripture, "God is not a man, that he should lie, nor a son of man, that he should change his mind. Does he speak and then not act? Does he promise and not fulfill" (Num 23:19)? Keep holding and speaking the promises of God.

- **"I will mold to your promise."** Learning to take aim and flame requires that we choose to pattern our flame after Jesus Christ who "entrusted himself" to God (1 Pet 2:23). In Romans 12:3, we're reminded that God molded us with a "measure of faith." Therefore, we must realize faith is a good deposit that God has entrusted us with, and we must "guard" it (2 Tim 1:14). Like Mary and Martha, if we will just believe, we will see the glory of God (John 11:40). We must stay put with God's agenda to see the culmination of His cultivation in our garden of dreams. Though the vision tarries, "wait for it; it will certainly come and will not delay" (Hab 2:3). We must keep molding our mind to a heart of gratitude as we wait upon the Lord.

- **"I will be sold out to your promise."** Does God revel in our commitment to staying the course to see His promises unfold? Does He "boast about your perseverance and faith in all the persecutions and trial you are enduring" (2 Thess 1:4)? Faith says, "God, I might not like this road, but I choose to be sold out to your will. I long to hear God say the words that Paul said to the church of the Thessalonians, "Your faith is growing more and more" (2 Thess 1:3). Job reminds us that, even though we are tested, there is a faith that will "come forth as gold" (Job 23:10).

So many times, we miss out on the blessings of faith. Let's take a look at some of the causes.

COMPLAINING

You will never learn to rely as long as you cry that you are going "to die in the desert" (Exod 14:12). If complaining had just been banned, the Israelites could have entered the Promised Land. In Numbers 16:41, we read how the Israelites "grumbled against Moses and Aaron," which caused them to want to give up. Complaining will erode and implode your faith in God. Complaining will force you to consider becoming a quitter who is bitter toward God. Philippians 2:14 reminds us to "do everything without complaining or arguing." Therefore, we will "shine like stars" (Phil 2:15).

ENTERTAINING

The enemy loves to entertain our minds with doubt. In Luke 24:38, Jesus asked his disciples an important question, "Why are you troubled, and why do doubts rise in your minds?" Today, Jesus is still asking us that same question. What are you asking God for: a baby, a faithful spouse, new promotions, a resurrected marriage, long-awaited healing, a new home, mended relationships, doors of opportunity to open, or a prodigal son or daughter to come home? God is not drawn to doubt but rather standout and knockabout faith! Is God using this chapter to commend your faith or confront it? In Matthew 14:31, Jesus confronts Peter by saying, "You of little faith." However, one chapter later, Jesus commends the faith of a mother when He says, "Woman, you have great faith" (Matt 15:28). May God find that kind of faith in us! Even through the haze, we must fix our gaze on the one who has prayed for all our faithless days. "But I have prayed for you, Simon, that your faith may not fail. And when you have turned back, strengthen your brothers" (Luke 22:32). When the heavens are like brass and there seems to be no other bypass, consider that thought. Jesus has prayed for you. When your problems are at their worst, go ahead and rehearse that verse over and over. Christ prayed for you to set your aim to greater faith. We must be deliberate in our protection of faith toward doubt.

Like mildew, doubt is a "fuzzy growth" that will affect the structure. In Leviticus 14:44-45, God was specific with Moses and Aaron about how to handle mildew. If a house was found to have "destructive mildew," it had to be torn down. That is exactly what we must do to the wall of doubt. Studies show mildew affects our breathing. And so it is with doubt. The breath of the Holy Spirit can't be activating where doubt is operating. Moreover, like mold, doubt will weaken our immune system. Satan intends to indent our lives with a mildew scent. As a flame, I can fight that indent when I "set my face like flint, and I know I will not be put to shame" (Isa 50:7).

When Christ returns, He will be looking for determined faith. Therefore, we must link our thoughts to faith. If we fail to link, we will shrink. Hebrews 10:37-38 gives us a clear picture of how God feels about shrinking. "He who is coming will come and will not delay. But my righteous one will live by faith. And if he shrinks back, I will not be pleased with him." We can learn from Peter that, when your faith starts shrinking, you start sinking.

Jesus told us that we would have tribulations in this world. However, we must see that tribulation as an entry point for a greater faith because He has already overcome that obstacle (John 16:33).

2 Timothy 4:7 reminds us to fight, finish, and keep the faith. The enemy will try everything he can to hinder your faith so you won't finish the race. Have you ever noticed how Satan always goes back to the old bag of tricks that once entangled you? It is time that we "run with perseverance the race marked out for us" (Heb 12:1). Let's surprise the enemy this time with our new flaming faith. Show him that his redundant fight only sets us up for abundant height where we can be the firelight for Christ that we long to be. God wants us to come to the place where the things that once caused us to trip just don't work anymore.

Like the apostles, our heart's cry must be for the Lord to "increase our faith" (Luke 17:5). Don't let doubt taint God's beautiful picture of your future. When life hits you the hardest and you feel yourself vexing, start flexing those muscles with flaming faith.

You know, I have found a great partner with faith. It's called patience. People whose names we find in the Faith Hall of Fame who accomplished great things for God's glory were men and women who understood the power of waiting. Long-suffering and waiting are a virtue that will not hurt you. Rather, they bring you to an intimate knowledge of the sweet

Holy Spirit that you wouldn't have otherwise known. Proverbs 14:29 says, "A patient man has great understanding."

Noah waited many days. Moses waited for a miracle, and he was amazed. David waited with lots of praise. Hannah waited in spite of delays. Shadrach, Meshach, and Abednego waited and were pulled from the blaze. Jesus has waited in spite of betrays, disobeys, and runaways.

Before closing out this chapter today, I want to look at two faith-filled Js.

1. **Genesis 37-50: Joseph.** Whenever I face adversity, I think of Joseph and say to myself, "Tonya Bennett, don't you dare quit on your it." Would you agree that Joseph's "it" consisted of a split, pit, hit, and a sit? He experienced a split from his family and home as he was thrown in a pit. Then, if that weren't enough to try his faith, he was hit by lies from Potiphar's wife and had to sit in prison and wait for his dreams to come to fruition. For thirteen years, Joseph spent his life as an Egyptian slave and a prisoner. Yet, Joseph continued to grow on tiptoe faith that God would turn his "it" into good (Gen 50:20). Every time I read the story of Joseph's life, I'm reminded that the dreams God has given me are not mine. They are His. My job is to be a flame that aims for Faith's Hall of Fame. I must remain confident that God will bring all my dreams that connect to the harvest to complete fulfillment.

2. **Exodus 2: Jochebed.** This woman has got to be one of my favorite mothers in the Bible. The birth pains of Moses were just the beginning of Jochebed's exertion of energy. This woman pushed past Pharaoh. She pushed past crocodiles in the river. She pushed past the screams of other Hebrew mothers whose cries of their murdered sons rang in her ears. She pushed past darkness and doubt until faith exploded. Then, with all that was within her, Jochebed placed the life of her little son, Moses, in God's hands. She embarked and pushed an ark toward its destiny. What were the results of her great faith? An entire race experienced freedom! With an outcome like that, how could we ever hold back on trusting God with great faith?

More and more, I am being drawn to the attitude of the father in Mark 9:24 who exclaimed, "I do believe; help me overcome my unbelief!" Growing in faith is a continual process.

As you are drawn to flame on, may you continue to seek "a faith and knowledge resting on the hope of eternal life, which God, who does not lie, promised before the beginning of time" (Titus 1:2). God wants us to live with an aim that empowers others with a feverish faith filled with passion, trust, and confidence in Christ. According to Luke 18:8, Jesus is coming back in search of persistent faith. "However, when the Son of Man comes, will he find faith on earth?" Faith is a gift (Eph 2:8). Satan would like nothing better than to sift that gift. However, I challenge you to use your gift to lift those who drift far from the cross.

Aren't you glad faith doesn't go out of date? An exclamation of faith can activate, captivate, elevate, motivate, and invigorate any dimly burning wick. And that does aggravate the enemy.

There have been so many things in my life that I have prayed about and knew they were in God's will, yet I couldn't see anything happening. Yes, I became very frustrated, but God remained patient with me. One day, God quieted my spirit while reading Hebrews 6:12 as He reminded me, "Faith and patience inherit what has been promised."

Let me just end by reminding you of something very important. If you want to be a candle with an awesome smell, you must dwell and wait well. Then you will excel from the pasture to the palace.

Your fire will spread as you move ahead . . . with extreme faith!

BIBLE STUDY IDEAS

CONNECT

Everyone plays Mountain Faith. Divide groups into two teams. Align a walkway space about four feet wide by twenty feet long. Designate a start and finish line. Randomly place four pieces of construction paper along the walkway. The paper should read "MOUNTAIN." The first person in line is the guide. He represents Christ, who sees the mountain ahead. The second person is the walker who must take each step by faith with his eyes closed as he listens to the words of the guide. It is the guide's job to aim the person to the finish line. The walker must follow the guide's voice who is quoting 2 Corinthians 5:7. "We live by faith, not by sight." When the walker gets close to the construction paper labeled

"MOUNTAIN," the guide must help the walker step over the paper without touching it by only shouting the word "MOUNTAIN FAITH." If the walker touches the paper labeled "MOUNTAIN," he must go back to the start line. Once the second person reaches the finish line, he must run back to the start line, where he now becomes the guide for the next person and so on. First team to cross all mountains with words of FAITH is the winner!

DIRECT
Share with your group a highlighted thought that ministers to you.

REFLECT
- What were some of the decisions that allowed Abraham to be among the Faith Hall of Fame? How can you relate to some of his decisions?
- Put Hebrews 11:1 in your own words.
- According to Romans 10:17, how can one develop his faith?
- Finish this sentence as it speaks to you personally: Faith helps me look beyond _____.
- How has faith affected, changed, or created something new in your life?
- Pick two adjectives to complete this sentence about yourself. At this point in my life, my faith is _____ and _____. Explain why.
- When others walk into your home or area of work, how can they identify your faith in Christ?

COLLECT
Research the following scriptures: Matthew 17:20, Mark 11:22-24, and Colossians 1:3-6. How will these scriptures help you to flame on with great faith?

AFFECT
Take the time to get with an accountability partner. Talk about a "mountain situation" that is in your life or maybe a friend's life. Agree together in faith for God's will to be done in this situation.

Love is kindled in a flame, and ardency in its life. Flame is the air which true Christian experience breathes. If feeds on fire; it can withstand anything rather that a feeble flame; but when the surrounding atmosphere is frigid or lukewarm, it dies, chilled and starved to its vitals. True prayer must be aflame.

E. M. Bounds

CHAPTER 12

Never Be the Same

Congratulations! You have made it to the last chapter. As I would say to my kindergarteners, "Give yourself a big pat on the back and say, 'I'm good stuff!'" Let's celebrate, shall we? Come with me for a minute to the celebration table. Let's sit down and take in the moment with Jesus.

The cake is angled at your space. A smile is wide on Abba Father's face. He is one proud Father, you know. He sees what only a parent sees in the face of celebration, growth. I hope something in this book has stretched you to a deeper desire to pursue the blue flame. Your desire to aim and flame is huge to God.

I sincerely hope you have found this book to be an energetic stirring. We should wake up every morning with an expectancy to be a greater light for Christ. Jesus specifically tells us in John 8:12 that, when we follow Him, we "will never walk in darkness, but will have the light of life."

God wants His light to shine in our hearts to "give us the light of the knowledge of the glory of God in the face of Christ" (2 Cor 4:6). I pray a passionate injection of His ardent affection will fill you. May you have a holy confidence that God will prevail over every detail that tries to assail your flame.

You can take this to the spiritual bank. The enemy has pinned a seductive aim next to your name. Satan doesn't want you drawn to fullness in Christ. He desperately wants to blow away your seeds of truth. But God is fiercely passionate about your insistent willpower to cross the finish line with a torch of holy fire in your hand.

Flaming friend, you must be prepared for resistance as you celebrate the distance that your flame has grown in Christ. Don't ever settle for the bench or choose to quench the "new thing" God wants to do in your life (Isa 43:19). Stir that zesty desire and "do no put out the Spirit's fire" (1Thess 5:19). It is also very important that you don't rely on yesterday's supply. It's too great of a risk not to daily whisk up fresh excitement. If your fire isn't stirred, your vision may become blurred.

The world has seen enough of goof. It's time to show them proof that one can really be a devout flame. Live such a life of glow that people go, "Whoa! I want to serve your God! I want to experience joy like that!"

DON'T GET OFF TRACK!

I believe strongly in five important disciplines that will help keep you on track. I pray that someone who really wants to thrive will take a dive into applying these five to their daily walk:

- **Obey** God's leading and aim for a life of holiness and reverence to God. May you be drawn to an obedient love that follows Christ with all your heart, mind, soul, and spirit.
- **Pray** daily to your Heavenly Father who longs to reveal secrets to you about your name. He will help you avoid the game of the enemy so you can stop any encroachment of sin that wants to destroy you.
- **Display** God's fame and make the mounted statement of your life declare, "Bring God glory." Live a life that makes Christ's name famous.
- **Stay** connected to the light source through the Word. As we place God's map in our lap, we will take aim and flame with an adventurous ride.
- Finally, be a **tray** that shouts, "Hooray!" when given the opportunity to serve the needs of others. 1 Peter 4:10 encourages us to use our gifts to serve others.

God has commissioned us to witness to others "to open their eyes, in order to turn them from darkness to light, and from the power of Satan to God, that they may receive forgiveness of sins" (Acts 26:18). As we cooperate with God's plan, He will use our witness to "snatch others from the fire and save them" (Jude 1:23).

The Bible tells us in Hebrews 12:29 that our "God is a consuming fire." I believe the fire is searching . . . searching . . . searching . . . for a room to consume and groom to be an atomic boom of fire! Will you be the available one?

Flame Pass the Attack

I truly pray that your fire of determination will never be the same. When frustration seems to be so great, just keep quoting Psalm 18:28, "You, O LORD, keep my lamp burning."

Do not allow your past to torment, or you will become dormant. God wants to give you a new song so "many will see and fear and put their trust in the LORD" (Ps 40:3). Your purpose is not to regress but to bless. We must stand tall and be a lighthouse to all who may not be able to see in the dark.

When you feel weak, keep your eyes on the strong peak, Jesus Christ. When you feel small, keep your eyes on His call on your life. Be tough and don't allow circumstances to snuff out your light.

Don't Get Slack

One thing God has to remind me of over and over is to refuse to become slack even when I can't see my life's impact on others. Just think about Paul. He never saw you or me. Yet that prison writing man increased our span of knowledge through so many books of the Bible. What if God never chooses to show you just how many people you have touched or affected? Will you still be drawn to take aim and flame? I hope you've got zest with a loud answer, "Yes!"

So many people haven't made up their minds to flame on because "the god of this age has blinded the minds of unbelievers, so that they cannot see the light of the gospel of the glory of Christ, who is the image of God" (2 Cor 4:4). Let me encourage you of this. If you stick to God's law, His favor will draw others to your flame for Him.

According to iwise.com, Oliver Wendell Holmes said, "A moment's insight is sometimes worth a life's experience." I pray the message of this book stirs you to be a bubbling brook with a deep fountain of wisdom to share with others (Prov 18:4).

I hope you are more determined than ever to show the enemy that what he has intended to use in your life as stress will just press you closer to the Father. We must choose to be God-focused and stop whining while God does the refining with our flaming candles.

Speaking of candles, have you ever thought about the connection between the love of Christ and a candle? They captivate, illuminate, activate, motivate, and radiate. They also help you to celebrate and communicate.

As we close this book, I pray you can see evidence in your life where you've become more unified, intensified, and electrified to make sure God is glorified in every area of your life.

God longs to bless His people. Psalm 89:15 specifically tells us that we will be blessed as we walk in the light of His presence. I pray we will become a unified body that walks in that flaming light.

Jesus even prayed for you and me to see the power of unity in John 17:23. "May they **be** brought to complete **unity** to let the world know that you sent **me**." Hey, did you catch Jesus's rhyme in my bold print?

Flaming one, your flame is your missile. Who will dare to bristle and flame on? Just "as fire consumes the forest or a flame sets the mountains ablaze," we can affect those around us for all eternity (Ps 83:14). If you really want to glow, minister out of the overflow of your personal experience of God's unfathomable love. Don't ever lay down your sword for "now you are light in the Lord" (Ep 5:8). You will enjoy life to the hilt when you choose to tilt toward God's purposes. The blaze you see is the blaze you will be! So aim with a sharp eye . . . and flame high!

BIBLE STUDY IDEAS

CONNECT

Play the Bingo Game. The group leader should have already created a five by five table with either funny, interesting, or serious facts written in each box. For example, facts might say: I like spinach, I have never been on a cruise, and so forth. Participants must go around and find someone who has or has not experienced this. They must get a signature for each square. You may win horizontally, vertically, or diagnostically. The first person who gets a full row of five signatures is the winner.

Direct
Share with your group a highlighted thought that ministers to you.

Reflect
- Which chapter has impacted you the most? Why?
- Psalm 56:13 encourages us to "walk before God in the light of life." How can we set aim to flame in our walk?
- What specific things must we do if our flame begins to flicker?
- Over the past few months of this study, what kind of changes have taken place in your thinking, attitude, view, and relationships that is pushing you closer and closer to the blue flame?
- Our flames should be aimed for the Harvest. Using the letters in the word "harvest," make a list of things that will not be in hell, like "hope," to remind yourself how important it is to flame on for Jesus. Then make a list of things that will be in heaven that will encourage you to take aim and flame until Christ calls you home.

What is Not in Hell?

H
A
R
V
E
S
T

What is Awaiting Us in Heaven?

H
A
R
V
E
S
T

- Nudge three people and say, "I'm going to take aim and flame for Christ like never before!"

COLLECT

Share one of your own favorite Bible scriptures with your group, and share how it has encouraged you.

AFFECT

As a group, join hands and form a unity circle. Pray that every member in your group will continue to aim and to flame with greater intensity. As a group, pray for our nation, families, friends, and churches to be deeply drawn to take aim and flame for Christ.

Other books written by Tonya Buck Bennett include *The Fabric of a Passionate Parent* and *The Mother Who Weaved an Ark*. You can invite Tonya to speak at your women's event by visiting her Web site at www.flame4him.com or contacting her by e-mail at flame4him@gmail.com.